Broadcasting, Society and Policy in the Multimedia Age

'08

Andrew Graham and Gavyn Davies

⁾01

UNIVERSITY *of*
UP **JL**
LUTON PRESS

British Library Cataloguing in Publication Data
A catalogue record for this page is available from the British Library
ISBN 1 86020 550 X

Broadcasting, Society And Policy In The Multimedia Age is the third in a series of public policy reports commissioned by the BBC.

The first two reports were:
Paying for Broadcasting (1992, Methuen) edited by Tim Congdon; and
The Cross Media Revolution: Ownership and Control (1995, John Libbey Media) by Tim Congdon, Andrew Graham, Damian Green and Bill Robinson.

The views in this book are, like in the two previous reports, those of the authors themselves, not of the BBC.

Andrew Graham is grateful to support from the ESRC's Media Economics and Culture Programme (Research Grant L126251017). We would also like particularly to thank Patricia Hodgson for her many perceptive comments and Stephen Mulhall who contributed at an earlier stage to our thinking about citizenship and community. Thanks are also due to Michael Bacharach, Thomas Gallagher, Peggotty Graham, Joseph Raz and Adam Swift. The usual disclaimers apply.

Published by

John Libbey Media
Faculty of Humanities, University of Luton,
75 Castle Street, Luton, Bedfordshire LU1 3AJ
Telephone: +44 (0)1582 743297
Facsimile: +44 (0)1582 743298
E-mail: ulp@luton.ac.uk

Printed in Great Britain by Whitstable Litho Ltd, Whitstable, Kent, UK

Contents

Executive Summary

Digital technology is revolutionising broadcasting. It makes possible a multiplicity of channels, interactive television, subscription TV and pay-per-view; indeed the scope to sell programmes just like many other goods and services. In this new world what is the role for broadcasting policy? Does the expansion of delivery systems mean that broadcasting will become a highly competitive market with both less *scope* for and little *need* for public policy beyond the minimal regulation necessary to protect standards of taste and decency? Or does the public interest require more than this? If so, what form should UK policy take in a world in which satellites increasingly broadcast from outside the UK and the Internet operates globally?

Our answer to these questions proceeds in two stages. First, we consider public policy and second the financing of the public policy that we recommend.

Public Policy

In the case of public policy we show that:

- The new technology creates strong pressures towards a broadcasting industry which is not competitive, but where *audiences are fragmented and yet ownership is concentrated.* This is because *high* quality multimedia content is expensive to produce, but relatively cheap to edit or to change and trivially cheap to reproduce. It therefore has high fixed costs and low marginal costs – the natural creators of monopolies.

- High quality material can still be produced and yet cost very little *per unit* provided that it reaches a large number of people (exploiting economies of scale) and/or provided that it is used in a wide variety of different formats (exploiting economies of scope), but the exploitation of these economies of scale and scope imply concentration of ownership.

- Thus, while one source of monopoly, spectrum scarcity, has gone, it has been replaced with another – the natural monopoly of economies of scale and scope on the one hand plus the natural scarcity of talent on the other.

- In addition, bottlenecks in gateways mean that *particular* consumers may well become reliant on a *single* supplier. If so, it will be like being able to shop at Tesco, but *only at Tesco*.

Need because of over-concentration

The force of these arguments is that, instead of the appealing picture of free competition, there is a major danger that the new technology will replace public monopolies with private monopolies. Monopolies are *always* a matter for concern, but in a democratic society private monopolies in the media must be a matter for *special* concern. → *special value of information*

The case for active public policy does not, however, rest only on the possible presence of an over-concentrated broadcasting industry. Even if there were a

1

competitive market, it would not be desirable for *all* of broadcasting to be provided purely commercially. This is because of:

Market Failure

check if you mention this

- Information is difficult to sell normally (consumers do not know what they are buying until they have the information, but once they have this they no longer need to buy it).
- Television and radio can have adverse effects that are "external" to the market (e.g. amplifying violence in society).
- Quality broadcasting is a 'merit' good (just as with education or training or health checks, consumers, if left to themselves tend to buy less than is in their own long term interests).

Thus, without positive pressure in the system, there is a real danger that broadcasting, instead of expanding our horizons, will "dumb us down".

Citizenship and Community

- As citizens we all have rights to core information about our own society. This is not something the market would provide.
- As members of a community we have views about society that cannot be captured just in our buying and selling. The Bertelsmann Foundation, for example, found that in ten countries surveyed people expected and wanted "socially responsible television".
- Our collective and individual capacities for imagination and achievement are affected by "the company we keep". Broadcasting is today part of this company. The communications system we, as a society, choose and the quality of the content that it carries will therefore be an important influence on the social values and concerns of the communities of the twenty first century.

Democracy

- It is a basic principle of a democratic society that votes should not be bought and sold. This alone is sufficient justification for broadcasting not being entirely commercial.
- The creation and sustenance of 'common knowledge' (what everyone knows that everyone knows) is a vital element in the functioning of democracy. In order to be *agreed*, solutions have to be based on a common understanding of the situation. Common knowledge is therefore a *pre-condition* of many coordination problems in democratic societies. Such 'common knowledge' is not well guarded by commercial markets.

Industrial Policy

- It is not the private market which has given the UK a successful broadcasting industry.
- By a clever mix of the public and the private, the UK has managed to generate for itself a "comparative advantage" in broadcasting. The UK's success has been led by the BBC and is the result of extensive investment in talent over many years. It would be foolish now to throw this away.

The implication of these arguments is that the market *on its own* cannot produce the full benefits of the new technology. Equally the deficiencies in the market cannot be filled just by negative regulation.

- The technical change of the 1990s with satellites increasingly broadcasting from outside the UK, with the Internet operating globally and with more intense commercial pressures makes regulation *less* effective.
- Rules are not appropriate for judging quality (and quality, by definition, cannot be measured – if it could, it would be quantity).
- Rules can only stop the undesirable, they cannot promote the desirable – it was not, for example, regulation that produced public libraries or world class universities or the National Trust.

What public policy therefore requires is a *positive* force that would:

- act as a counterweight to the private concentration of ownership;
- deliver *national coverage* so as to counteract fragmentation of audiences;
- provide a "centre of excellence" which both makes and broadcasts programmes;
- be large enough to influence the market and so act as the guarantor of quality;
- widen choice both now and in the future by complementing the market through pursuit of public service purposes.

The best way to provide this positive pressure is via public service broadcasting *SoS* (not as a substitute to the commercial sector but as a complement to it).

The conclusion of this part of the argument is that, while a public service broadcaster, such as the BBC, has no *right* to exist, there are *purposes for its existence*. Moreover, contrary to the conventional wisdom, the new technology *increases, rather than decreases,* the need for such a broadcaster.

Finance

If public service broadcasting remains essential to broadcasting policy, how then should it be financed? Any system should:

- allow consumers to make a direct link between the benefits they receive, and the outlays they make;
- be paid by all (since all will receive it);
- be at a flat rate so that there is a direct link between the level of the service received by everyone, and the level of the charge made on everyone;
- ideally show some form of income-elasticity so that receipts grow at least in line with nominal GDP;
- be subject to minimum interference from the government of the day;
- be relatively easy to collect, enforce and administer.

The form of finance which best meets most of these requirements remains the licence fee. However, tying the licence fee to the RPI is mistaken.

- The RPI has no buoyancy.
- BBC revenue increases more slowly than BBC costs (which are primarily labour).
- The result is that the BBC will lose market share year by year.
- If uprated just by the RPI the BBC's market share would probably decline to less than 40 per cent by the year 2000 and to below 30 per cent by 2010.

The BBC probably needs to maintain a market share of at least one third.

- A share of 30 per cent or more is probably needed for it to fulfill its crucial "quality setting" role.
- Below 25-30 per cent the licence fee may become unsustainable.

It follows that the method of up-rating must be changed if the "quality-guarantee" is to be achieved – if we want a society in which the demand for both information and education are rising faster than national income, then the public provision of these should also rise.

- In the short term the licence fee should be related, not to the RPI, but to the increase in unit labour costs in the private service sector (probably about 0.5 per cent per annum above the RPI)
- In the longer term, when an adequate index has been constructed, it should be linked to the increase in unit costs in broadcasting.

In the meantime two other methods for setting the licence fee should be considered:

- a higher licence fee for digital TVs;
- a "site" licence with a higher charge for more than one TV.

The most fundamental points of all are:

- The new technology which reinforces both commercial pressures and globalisation does not remove the case for public service broadcasting – on the contrary it *increases* the need for it.
- The need to guarantee quality should determine the scale of the future financial arrangements – not the other way around.
- The position of the BBC is not symmetrical – it could easily be undermined, but once undermined it would be difficult to replace.
- A successful public broadcasting service, still admired both at home and abroad, should not be thrown away. Seventy five years of public broadcasting culture could be destroyed far more easily than it could be re-created.

I   Introduction

Broadcasting is currently undergoing the biggest change since the arrival of television. Five years ago cable and satellite were minuscule and broadcasting was totally dominated by four channels. No-one, beyond a handful of research workers, had even heard of the Internet, let alone thought that it had anything to do with television. Today cable and satellite channels are booming, digital television is about to begin and we stand, we are told, on the verge of an Information Society with broadcasting, computing, publishing and telecommunications converging into a single media market. Indeed it has been argued that this change, which is occurring on a global scale, is the most significant development in communications since the introduction of the printing press by Gutenberg more than half a millennium ago.

The result of this change is that broadcasting is moving – and moving rapidly – into an apparently far more competitive and market driven environment. A central question for broadcasting policy is therefore how well this burgeoning market will serve the public interest. Undoubtedly the extension of the market will expand choice and the increase in competition will put downward pressure on costs. Both of these would be welcome developments, but will the market also foster a democratic environment, provide the information to which all citizens are entitled and extend, rather than diminish, the tastes, experiences and capacities of individuals? If not, how are these public interest goals to be achieved, especially in the more deregulated and more open environment that the global revolution in communications is producing? In short, what should broadcasting policy now be trying to do and how is this to be achieved?

EFFECTS

QUOTE THIS

1⁰ – new technology changing broadcasting environment

Re: NEW MARKET –

II   The Fundamental Arguments

The best way of starting to think about what is desirable for broadcasting is to begin by addressing the fundamental arguments about the role of the market. The central claim made in favour of the market is that the new technology means that television and radio programmes *can be made and sold just like any other commodity and that this is desirable*. Note that this argument contains two separate propositions:

(a) that programmes *can* be sold commercially, and
(b) that it is *desirable* that this should occur.

Note also that the second does not automatically follow from the other. For example, it is perfectly possible to buy and sell babies, but most of us find this morally repugnant and, at least in the UK, there are laws to prohibit it. This may seem an extreme case, but it should not be assumed that this makes it an isolated one. In reality there are a multiplicity of situations in which society aims to influence the market so that people buy more or less than would otherwise be the case. Thus society tries to ban some products all together (e.g. drugs or child pornography). In others it tries to limit consumption either via regulation (e.g. the distribution of alcohol) or through taxation (e.g.on tobacco). It also influences consumption in a positive direction by promoting the use of some goods through laws (e.g. the requirement to wear seat belts) or by subsidies (e.g. grants to promote energy conservation) or by direct public provision (eg health care via the NHS).

The point about all these examples is that they remind us that, while the market functions extremely well for allocating some goods, it does not do so for all goods. The essential public policy question is therefore:

> Does new technology make broadcasting just like many others goods that are sold successfully via the market or does it have any special characteristics which make this either impossible or undesirable?"

The case in favour of thinking that broadcasting is just like many other goods sold commercially was put forcibly a decade ago by Peter Jay in evidence to the Peacock Committee. He regarded broadcasting in the age of new technology as simply "electronic publishing". He therefore argued that broadcasting, once it came fully of age, would require no public service presence nor any regulation save that of maintaining standards of taste and decency.[1] The Peacock Committee was much taken with the analogy and in particular with the much more competitive environment that this suggested. They also added historical comparisons with publishing. They argued that printing and publishing had been similarly fettered with unnecessary constraints when first invented, but had eventually been emancipated. In addition they regarded such emancipation as highly desirable since they believed, in accordance with the First Amendment to the US Constitution, that there should be

---

1. Peacock Committee para 477.

freedom of speech.[2] Indeed the Peacock Committee went so far as to state that the enlargement of freedom of choice which they saw as following from the development of a full broadcasting market ought to be positively required by anyone interested in promoting "public service".

Although the Peacock Committee reported a decade ago, their position has set the tone of most subsequent debate. Many recent pronouncements have echoed their themes. Sources as disparate as Rupert Murdoch, Gerald Kaufman,[3] the *New Statesman*, the *Economist* and the think tank, DEMOS, have all *welcomed* the expansion of the commercial sector and the extension of consumer choice. The ability to sell broadcasting, apparently like many other goods, has also made many question the need for public service broadcasting. This is now often seen as either unnecessary (spectrum scarcity has gone so there is no longer any case for public control), or as undesirable (because public service broadcasting is paternalistic), or as an anachronism (in the new world of competition and convergence, broadcasting policy should reflect the needs of industrial policy not the desires of a cultural elite), or as unsustainable (as other broadcasters expand people's willingness to pay the licence fee will disappear).

There is no doubt that spectrum scarcity is disappearing and that, as a result, a much larger number of channels is now possible. This is desirable. Nevertheless, two questions remain: will the market produce all that is desired and, if not, what other forms of public policy will be required?

In what follows it will be shown that, when the position is analysed carefully, the goals that most people want from broadcasting will *not* be achieved by the market *on its own*. In particular we will argue that the way in which both the issue of choice and the analogies with publishing have been formulated by Peacock and by almost everyone else who has followed these lines of argument is mistaken. As a result we shall show not only that a degree of regulation continues to be needed, but also that this regulation can be – and needs to be – complemented by an important component of public service broadcasting.

In summary the argument is as follows:

First, we show in Section III that, while the new technology undoubtedly makes it possible to sell programmes, that same technology also creates strong pressures towards a broadcasting industry in which *audiences are fragmented and yet whose ownership is concentrated*. Thus, instead of the appealing picture of free competition, there is a major danger of replacing public monopolies with private monopolies. Monopolies are *always* a matter for concern, but in a democratic society private monopolies in the media must be a matter for *special* concern.

Second, we show in Sections IV to VII that, even if the market in broadcasting were to be competitive, it would still be undesirable for *all* of broadcasting to be

---

2. Peacock Committee para 548.

3. The Chairman of the House of Commons Committee on Broadcasting.

provided purely commercially. (Of course over the next decade there will be an enormous expansion of commercial channels and this is to be welcomed, but the argument here is that this must be complementary to public service broadcasting not a replacement for it.)

In brief there are four reasons why a broadcasting market run on purely commercial terms would be undesirable:

1. **Market Failure**

    Eonomic analysis suggests strong grounds for thinking that private markets in broadcasting, good as they will be in some areas, will fail on their own to produce the overall quality of broadcasting that consumers either individually or collectively would desire. The two most important reasons why this happens are first, that broadcasting can have adverse "external effects"(e.g.amplifying violence in society) and second, that good broadcasting is a 'merit' good (just as with education or training or checking on their health, consumers, if left to themselves tend to buy less than is in their own long term interests).

2. **Citizenship and Community**

    The market, being by definition the mere aggregation of individual decisions, takes no account of the community and of the complex relations between citizenship, culture and community. In particular, the fragmentation of audiences that purely commercial broadcasting may produce could undermine both communities and cultures by limiting our shared experiences.

3. **Democracy**

    In a democratic society it is undesirable that the mass media should be entirely in private control (especially if such control were concentrated in few hands). Moreover, we show that the creation and sustenance of 'common knowledge' (what everyone knows that everyone knows) is a vital element in the functioning of democracy and this 'common knowledge' is not well guarded by commercial markets.

4. **Industrial Policy**

    It is not the private market which has given the UK a broadcasting industry which is widely regarded as the best in the world. In the language of economists, by a clever mix of the public and the private, the UK has managed to generate for itself a "comparative advantage" in broadcasting and it would be foolish now to throw this away.

Showing that commercial broadcasting would fail in a variety of ways does not thereby establish that there should be public service broadcasting. It would still be possible, at least in principle, to regulate the market through a variety of rules. In Section XIII therefore "rules-based" interventions are compared with various forms of public service broadcasting. Here it is shown that some "rules-based" intervention would be necessary but not sufficient.

Most important of all, this section shows that in each of the four areas of concern (market failure and quality, citizenship and fragmentation, democracy and common knowledge, and industrial policy and comparative advantage) public service broadcasting is a highly effective form of intervention. Moreover it is a form of intervention that achieves what regulation cannot. In particular, the direct provision of public service broadcasting creates the possibility for a *positive* influence on the system (filling gaps, setting standards and generating pressures towards high quality). As a result this achieves ends which rules, being by their very nature *negative*, never can. Finally, this section shows that the globalisation which is one of the consequences of the new technology, reduces the power of national authorities. As a result rules-based intervention will be *less* effective than in the past. Thus, the new technology increases, *not* decreases, the importance of public service broadcasting.

Having set out the case for structuring the commercial market by setting it in a context that includes a fundamental component of public service broadcasting, the paper considers (in Sections IX and X) the ways in which such public service broadcasting should be funded. After reviewing in Section XI what has happened to public funding in the past, the empirical consequences over the next decade of a range of alternative regimes for public funding are set out (Sections XII and XIII). Section XIV summarises and concludes.

III   The Effects of the New Technologies on Broadcasting

The impact of the new technology on broadcasting is dramatic. In 1982, after C4 started, there were four channels. By 1990 there were twenty channels and by the autumn of 1996, seventy four channels. Within a few years digital broadcasting will make this two hundred or more. Meanwhile, springing up alongside this is the totally new world of the Internet bringing with it the scope for interactive television and the capacity to order whatever programme one wants, whenever one wants, wherever one wants.

Thus, so the argument goes, there will be intense competition between delivery systems, between channels and between broadcasters. However, while it is correct that the number of *channels* will change in this way it does not follow that the number of *broadcasters* will change correspondingly. When the situation is examined more carefully in terms of (a) production, (b) delivery and (c) consumption, it is far more likely both that broadcasting will remain highly concentrated in the hands of few large owners and that *particular* consumers will become reliant on a *single* supplier. It will be like being able to shop at Tesco, but *only at Tesco*.

Economies of Scale

Take *production*: here two factors will generate highly concentrated broadcasting. First, both the making and broadcasting of radio and more especially television programmes has exceptionally high fixed costs. At the same time they have very low, in many cases zero, marginal costs. Almost by definition, to "broadcast" is to say that it costs no more to reach extra people. Economists describe this phenomenon as either "economies of scale" or as the gap between "first copy" and "second copy". When economies of scale are significant (ie when this gap is large), entry to the market is difficult and firms tend to be concentrated.

Against this some argue that the new technology is lowering these entry costs and that the market will therefore become more competitive. With one exception, the Internet (which is considered further below), this is much less true than, at first, it seems. It is true that the digital revolution is making cameras and recording equipment much smaller and in some cases cheaper (or more sophisticated for the same price). New technology has also allowed much simpler, and so faster, processing and editing. In the longer term it may even save on sets (for example by using computer generated 'virtual' backcloths). Nevertheless the fundamental point is that most costs are not equipment but people – and not just individual people, but *teams* of people (writers, designers, performers, etc) all working together. In aggregate these are considerable – especially for programmes of any quality. The *average* cost per hour of a BBC production is more than £100,000; a current affairs programme approximately £175,000 and drama programmes approach half a million. Typical ITV costs are some twenty-five per cent higher. Similarly the fixed costs of transmission, whether in renting space on satellites or in establishing digital terrestrial broadcasting facilities or in installing fibre optic cables to the home, rule out all except the very large.

The likely cost to the BBC of establishing digital terrestrial services is not yet known, but even establishing digital transmission for the existing services seems likely to be over £50 million (and the cost of providing digital presentation to the viewer will push these costs even higher). The cost of putting up a broadcasting satellite is so large that Rupert Murdoch told Andrew Neil that he was "betting the company on it".[4]

Most important is that for quality programmes the real cost of *content* is rising not falling. All the discussion of technical change in the delivery of programmes ignores the fact that *talent and desirable content is scarce*. Moreover, it is the technical change in delivery which is bringing this scarcity to the fore. The combination of more channels with multimedia companies that are increasingly operating on a global basis is generating far greater competition for services which are in short supply. In effect an economic rent (a payment for scarcity) which in the past was suppressed by the bargaining power of the small number of broadcasters is now being revealed. The result is that over the last six years the average cost of the top 100 contributors to UK television has risen *in real terms* by nearly 7 percent per annum (or by more than 50 percent in total) and, on average, between 1990 and 1995 total talent costs for sitcoms, drama, features and documentaries rose by approximately 5 per cent per annum in real terms.[5] Sports rights illustrate the problem even more dramatically. Formula 1 Grand Prix which cost the BBC £2 million per annum during the years 1993-96 has now been sold to ITV for £12 million per annum and the television rights to the Summer Olympics increased from £59 million to £165 million. In the face of such figures it is hard to take seriously the idea that broadcasting can be a world of small competitors.

Economies of Scope

The second factor creating concentration is that, in addition to economies of scale, the new technology offers economies of scope. Such economies occur when activities in one area either decrease costs or increase revenues in a second area. New technology (in particular the digitisation of all information and the convergence that this is making possible) is greatly increasing this. For example, in the past newspapers and television stations were separate activities. Today, information gathered for a newspaper can be repackaged as a radio or television programme. Indeed, because digital information can be endlessly edited, copied, stored, retrieved, redesigned and merged with other information it can reappear in a multiplicity of formats.

Strong evidence that economies of scope plus scarcity of good content will produce concentration of ownership can already be seen. In particular, the digital revolution and the convergence it is creating is a major cause of the extraordinary global rush to multimedia mergers observed in recent years. Every one of the top

---

4.   Andrew Neil on Radio 4 on 1 December 1996.

5.   Voice of the Listener and Viewer, 1996.

seven multimedia firms in the world has in the last few years been buying, merging or being bought. In 1994 Viacom acquired Paramount and Blockbuster creating a company with a turnover of nearly £8 billion. In 1995 Disney took over Capital Cities/ABC in a deal worth $19 billion. Time Warner responded in 1996 by bidding for Turner Broadcasting (owner of the world's largest film and animation library) generating a company with total revenues of $20 billion.

Nor has the action all been American. Bertelsmann, the largest European audio-visual company with revenues of some $15 billion coming mostly from publishing, announced in April 1996 a merger of the TV subsidiary Ufa with CLT (Compagnie Luxembourgeoise de Telediffision) which will make it Europe's largest broadcaster; and both BSkyB and Kirch (one of the largest owners of copyright in Germany) have taken shares in DF1 (the first digital television service to be launched in Germany).

So powerful are the pressures towards convergence that even companies quite outside the multimedia world have been buying in. Seagram (the world second largest distiller) bought MCA from Matsushita in 1995 for just under $6 billion. In the same year Westinghouse, primarily an electrical goods company, bought CBS for $5.4 billion and in 1996 has bid $3.7 billion for Infinity Broadcasting. Similarly Phillips, the world's third largest electronics company, owns 75 per cent of Polygram, the world's number one music company, and maker amongst other things of *Four Weddings and a Funeral*, *Trainspotting* and *Dead Man Walking*, and in Procter and Gamble (best known as makers of detergents) formed a strategic alliance with Paramount Television (owned by Viacom).[6]

Also relevant is that the scale of these global mergers is considerably greater than that of even the largest UK multimedia firms. Time Warner or Disney or Bertelsmann all have turnovers that are five times or more greater than the BBC and ten to twenty times greater than the Mirror Group. Concentration of ownership is therefore already a fact not a speculation.

Delivery Systems and Gateways

Now consider *delivery*. It is clear here that the new technology is increasing the number of ways by which broadcasting can be delivered (satellite and cable have already been added and BT claims that in its trials in Ipswich an ordinary telephone line is sufficient to carry video on demand). In addition, digital technology means that the number of channels that can be carried by *each* of these means is also rising. Indeed in the digital world the concept of the channel might seem to be redundant – there is just a stream of bits which are first one programme and then another. At first glance competition in delivery therefore appears to be a real possibility.

In practice, however, the very technology that makes competition look likely also creates the conditions for proprietary control. The area of greatest concern is the set-top box through which which cable and satellite signals pass at the moment and through which in the future *all* digital signals will have to pass. If the signals were

6. Proctor and Gamble had an earlier small interest in sponsoring broadcasting – hence the term "soap operas".

from BBC, ITV or C4 and the programmes remained free at the point of use (or "free to air" as it is called) the set-top box would merely transfer digital signals to analogue. However, for "pay per view" the set-top box would also control access (as it does now for satellite and cable) and make sure that payment occurred. These Conditional Access Systems and Subscriber Management Systems (as they are known) thus represent a potentially extremely powerful "gateway".

Moreover digital technology will allow these gateways to be quite sophisticated. Once "channels", in the old sense, disappear, the gateway will be the means by which consumers select programmes (using what are called Electronic Programme Guides, EPGs). But these EPGs will do far more than select. They will soon allow access to a variety of "smart" features, such as automatically recording particular programmes, or finding programmes of a particular type and alerting the viewer. They may also become the means by which consumers "filter" programmes, for example, by choosing only to receive programmes that are below a certain rating for violence or sex or whatever.[7] All of this technology will sit in a single box (a box that will soon be incorporated directly into the TV) and, via an "applications programme interface (or API)", this box will control the television. What seems almost inevitable in these circumstances is that consumers will only be willing to buy a single box. If so, then, despite the increase in the number of delivery systems, there will only be a single point through which every digital channel from every broadcaster has to pass.

In the UK concern over the potential monopoly control of these gateways arises because of the position of BSkyB. At present there are numerous such boxes for cable TV reception since almost every cable company uses a different type. However, in the analogue satellite television market there is just a single conditional access system, VideoCrypt. This is owned by News Datacom, a subsidiary of Rupert Murdoch's News International which owns 40 percent of BSkyB, so any broadcaster wanting to use the VideoCrypt system must pay News Datacom for the service. In addition, out of the thirty channels available via satellite in the UK in 1996, twenty eight use Sky's subscription service. Moreover BSkyB is now a major part of British Digital Broadcasting, the group widely expected to be successful in its bid to broadcast digital terrestrial television. If this bid is successful it will be the first to launch digital set top boxes in 1998 and, as a result, will be in a dominant position.

In response to such criticism Sky have argued that other operators could establish satellite broadcasting or their own Subscriber Management Systems (SMS) and that no one applying to use VideoCrypt has ever been turned away. However, this position conveniently overlooks four counter objections.

These objections are seen most clearly when we consider the *consumer*. First, all the existing satellite dishes are set to receive Sky channels. The idea that customers would buy second aerials or point their existing aerials elsewhere is totally unrealistic. What consumers want (as Sky of course knows) is a single system offering the widest possible choice. Thus the existing situation gives the incumbent firm large advantages.

---

7. Technology now being tested for the Internet called Programme Interface Content Selector (PICS) allows consumers to check, via ratings offered by third parties, whether or not to receive particular material.

Second, a similar advantage accrues to having established a Subscriber Management System. There is nothing technologically complicated here, just (yet again) high fixed costs and low marginal costs providing natural barriers to entry. Third, what matters about the access of other broadcasters is not whether they were "turned away", but whether or not the prices they were quoted represented Sky's monopoly ownership of VideoCrypt – a quite different matter. Finally, anyone who controls the gateway also controls the agenda – what you see when you first switch on, where it is easiest to go next, what is drawn to your attention (and what is not) and what your TV does as its "default" setting.

Although so far little discussed, this power over the agenda may ultimately be the most important. As already noted, once digital television arrives "channels" will no longer exist. This is because many programmes may share the same spectrum. As a result viewers will need to select what they watch by using their hand sets and picking programmes from the display on the television (the "electronic programme guide"). In the age of the Information Superhighway when activities as diverse as shopping, banking, visiting an estate agent, consulting your doctor or taking your degree may all start (and in some cases end) with the TV, will consumers think it wise that the initial menus of choice should all be under the control of a single commercial firm? Of course, especially with careful packaging some consumers might not realise that this was the case, but the policy issue facing society would still be present.[8]

The Internet

So far it has been argued that the characteristics of production, content and delivery all suggest strong underlying pressures towards concentration and monopolisation. However, today's Information Superhighway (in the shape of the Internet) appears to offer a counter example. Millions of people are placing information on it every day and even greater millions are using it to retrieve information. It is therefore not at all monopolised. *However, far from this being counter evidence, this is the exception that proves the rule*. The Internet, at least at the moment, is not monopolised for three key reasons. First, the system was developed primarily by University research workers[9] totally committed to creating an open system – the whole philosophy of the Internet is that it should be capable of connecting to all systems anywhere.[10] Second, until 1994 academics users predominated and entry for them was particularly easy as most of them have their fixed costs supported by public funding. Third, and most important, the great majority of the content on the Internet is extremely cheap to produce. This is because the cost of collecting some kinds of information (most obviously personal information or personally created information) is very low, and because, psychologically, people appear to value self-promotion and/or participation (so labour costs are zero). But, and this is also central, being cheap much of the content available on the Internet is of abysmal quality.

---

8. Fuller discussion of these important issues can be found in Oftel (1996) and Graham (1997).

9. The initial researchers were working on projects for the US Department of Defence, who also provided the early funding, but the bulk of the research was in Universities or by people seconded from Universities.

10. The growth of Intranets, closed systems using Internet technology, may threaten this.

Of course there is some good material on the Internet, but the majority of the material that is better quality is there either because it has been well organised to attract advertising or because it has been produced by public or quasi-public bodies (universities, libraries, museums, etc). Most of the rest is poor precisely because it is cheap and because most of the new sources are not embedded within any stable institutional framework and/or are without the implicit codes of professionalism that characterise existing reputable sources of information. Indeed even the British Government fails in many cases to say when the information was first posted or when it was last revised. Much of the information on today's Information Highway is therefore misleading or hard to understand. There are, for example, plenty of "home pages" that have been left abandoned and many others where anyone with specialist knowledge can easily see that lists of information are incorrect, incomplete or out of date. As Dr. David Clarke of MIT and one of the architects of the Internet has remarked what is needed now is a layer of "editorship" to help users make sense of the "information soup".

In short the Internet is at the opposite end of the spectrum from mass market high quality multimedia broadcasting. In the digital age both the Internet and traditional broadcasting can, just, be described as "electronic publishing", but this catch-all phrase fails to draw the important distinctions between one medium which is personally addressable, usually received in private and is low cost and frequently low quality and another which is broadcast to a mass market, often received in public and which, if it is to be of high quality, will have high fixed costs. Of course there are already intermediate cases (such as CD-ROMs) and the new technology will spawn more, many more, but to say that we cannot therefore distinguish one from the other is as unhelpful as saying that because night shades imperceptibly into day we do not know the difference.

It should also be noted that we do not know how the Internet will develop. At the moment the multiplicity of sources predominates. However, in the longer term economies of scale and scope in the collection, organisation and dissemination of high quality information may apply to the Internet almost as much as to traditional broadcasting. For example, it is clear that some sites on the Net are already beginning to become better known. In this case the Internet itself might need to be thought of as two separate parts. One part being somewhat like conversations on the telephone and one part being somewhat like broadcasting, but with a reply channel thrown in.

Dilemmas for Public Policy: Concentration and Fragmentation

Whatever the outcome for the Internet, the central point, true both of today's broadcasting and tomorrow's Information Superhighway, is that *high* quality multimedia content is expensive to produce in the first place and yet, once commissioned and created, relatively cheap to edit or to change and trivially cheap to reproduce. In other words, as already stated, it has high fixed costs and low marginal costs – and these are the natural creators of monopolies.

Here we have a critical dilemma for public policy. High quality material can still be produced and yet cost very little *per unit* provided that it reaches a large number of people (exploiting economies of scale) and/or provided that it is used in a wide variety of different formats (exploiting economies of scope), but the exploitation of these economies of scale and scope imply concentration of ownership. Thus, even though the new technology has removed once source of monopoly, spectrum scarcity, it has replaced it with another, the natural monopoly of economies of scale.

How then should this potential concentration be tackled? Can it be left to the market or does it have to be regulated in one way or another, and, if so, how? We return to these questions below.

Another dilemma follows logically from the combination of economies of scale and scope on the one hand and a constrained audience on the other. More channels has *not* meant more time is being spent watching television. In 1995 in the UK the number of hours watched per person was twenty five. This is *identical* to what it was in 1980 before the arrival of either Channel 4, or cable or satellite. Thus more channels fragment audiences. The inevitable consequence is that the audience per channel or per programme falls and, given economies of scale, the average cost rises. This is *not* true for most goods and services that are allocated via the market place. A larger choice of restaurants or shoe shops or hotels does not lead to higher costs, in fact frequently the opposite as competition pushes costs down. The difference between these goods and services and broadcasting is that the former have much smaller fixed costs and variable costs are also significant. Thus minimum cost production is quite small, whereas minimum cost production in broadcasting is large. The result is that *choice has a cost in broadcasting* and this is a cost which is *not* normally faced elsewhere. Under "free market" conditions consumers will face a choice between a narrower range of cheaper (and yet still high quality) broadcasting and a broader range of more expensive and yet lower quality programmes.

The obvious response from those who advocate the expansion of commercial TV is that this is a choice that should be left to consumers. Why do otherwise? If some consumers want lots of choice and the consequence is that they pay more and yet, on average, receive lower quality, is that not up to them and does the market not correctly reflect their wishes? Surprising as it may seem, analysis suggests the opposite.

The reason that the individual choices via the market do not capture individual's wishes accurately is because of 'externalities'. These are the effects of one person's purchase on someone else, but which the market ignores. The effects may be either harmful, as in the case of traffic congestion arising from private car use, or beneficial as in the case of vaccinations – everyone benefits from the fact that *other* people are vaccinated. The existence of externalities means that left to itself the market produces too many car journeys and too few vaccinations (which is one reason why petrol is taxed particularly heavily and why there are public health programmes for vaccinations).

In the case being examined here the externalities arise because the person who migrates away from existing channels in favour of others imposes a cost on all those who do not move and this is a cost that the mover does not have to pay and so does not take into account. The situation is analogous to that of membership of a club. Clubs have common facilities, the costs of which have to be shared. As a result, if someone leaves all the remaining members face either higher charges or worse facilities or both. But this is not the optimal outcome. If the members who remain were able to organise themselves they would all be willing to offer the potential leaver a sum just below the extra costs that they would otherwise face in order to try the persuader to remain. If such side payments were on offer less people would decide to leave. However, in broadcasting it is impossible to organise in this way because it is too expensive to find them and to communicate with them (they are numerous, unknown and uncontactable). As a result a pure free market in broadcasting would be biased in favour of too much fragmentation of audiences (and, at the same time, too much concentration of ownership).

IV Other Market Failures in Broadcasting

Consumers and Market Failure

There is another set of 'externalities' which applies to broadcasting more than most other goods and services. These are not the direct result of fragmentation, but, like excessive fragmentation, they also threaten quality. These exist once we suppose, as both common sense and research suggests (a) that television has some influence upon the lifestyles, habits, interests, etc., of those who watch it and (b) that these habits, tastes, interests and sympathies have implications for those around us. Indeed, even just the *belief* that television affects behaviour is sufficient for externalities to exist. An elderly person may become more fearful of walking down the street at night if they believe that the portrayal of large amounts of irrational violence on TV encourages such behaviour, irrespective of whether in fact it does or not – the possible falseness of the belief does not alter the genuineness of the fear. In other words the television that is broadcast ought to reflect the preferences not only of those who watch it but also those affected by it indirectly – yet the market cannot do this. It follows that, if left just to the market, more "bad" TV (bad in the sense of being judged to have harmful side effects) and less "good" TV will be purchased than consumers in aggregate would have wished if they could have acted collectively.

A further reason why a broadcasting market would not work as well as that for many other goods and services is that markets do not work well where what is being sold is information or experience.[11] People do not know what they are "buying" until they have experienced it, yet once they have experienced it they no longer need to buy it! Of course it can be argued that in such information-based markets consumers are often willing to experiment by paying for the right to access a bundle of information with the chance that some might prove useful. But this argument does not remove the problem. If the right long-run choices are to be made, the cost of the initial experiments should only be the marginal cost of disseminating the information, and in the case of broadcasting this is zero.[12]

Third, and most important, the theory of choice on which the *economic* claim in favour of a free market in broadcasting rests relies on a fallacious assumption. This theory assumes that consumers know their own preferences. Indeed it operates as *if* people arrive in the world *already* fully formed. Although, strictly speaking, such an assumption is false everywhere, it may be a reasonable assumption for some goods and services – people undoubtedly do have different tastes and they can *find out* by

---

11. The seminal article was Arrow (1962).

12. It should be noted that the usual economic argument for charging for something (whether this is a 'price' or a 'subscription') does not apply to broadcasting because there is no question of anything being scarce. Broadcasts are a public good because one person's consumption does not compete with another person's consumption. It would therefore be perverse to insist that broadcasts become 'narrow-casts'.

experiment what meets their tastes. However, in broadcasting such an assumption is seriously flawed. Much of broadcasting exists to inform and educate us, but the process of learning and understanding the world is part of how our preferences are *formed*. They cannot therefore be taken as given in advance.

Those who advocate a free market in broadcasting discount both this and the preceding argument (about the costs of information) on the grounds that television unlike, say, a pension policy, is purchased every day, so any mistakes that a consumer may make can be quickly corrected. That much is true, but what is at issue here is both more subtle and more important. The point is that in the particular case of broadcasting consumers may be unavoidably myopic about their own long-term interests. Consumers cannot be other than ill informed about effects that broadcasting may have on them, *including effects on their preferences about television itself.* Moreover, such effects may well be spread out over a period of years after the present reception of broadcasting.

The point being made here is not that television may have great power for good or evil over society as a whole, but that television has the capacity either to cramp or to expand the knowledge, experience and imagination of *individuals*. Television fictions, Tim Mepham has said, "...can expand the viewer's sense of what is possible and enhance his or her vocabularies and repertoires of words, gestures and initiatives... *only if they are of high quality*" (emphasis added).[13] In other words, if all television is elicited by the market, there is a very real danger that consumers will under-invest in the *development* of their *own* tastes, their *own* experience and their *own* capacity to comprehend. This is not because consumers are stupid but because it is only in retrospect that the benefits of such investment become apparent.[14]

In technical terms, good quality broadcasting is what economists call a 'merit good'. It is analogous to eating sensibly or receiving preventative health care. No matter how much someone tells us in advance that we need it, the evidence is that, in general, we underinvest in it. In a free market in broadcasting where each item would have to be paid for at the point of use, this tendency to underinvest in watching those programmes which did not attract us at that moment would be greatly (and mistakenly) increased.

The arguments above have focused on how, seen from the standpoint of the *consumer* a pure market in broadcasting would have some drawbacks – possibly quite severe. Evidence from countries which have moved closest to pure markets in broadcasting, such as the USA, suggests that drawbacks are real, not just theoretical. Moreover, these concerns become larger when seen in the context of how the producers of broadcasting might behave.

---

13. Mepham (1989) p.67.

14. It should be noted that we distinguish "quality", which, by definition, cannot be measured, from "standards", which might be measurable.

Market Failures in Production

The danger that market driven broadcasting will lead to concentration has already been discussed, but there is a more general problem. In the particular case of the UK, there is a considerable body of evidence that over a long period many UK industries have failed in four related areas. They have taken too "short" a view;[15] they have not innovated sufficiently;[16] they have given insufficient attention to quality;[17] and they have failed to invest sufficiently in training.[18] The explanation of these failings is complex, but one factor pinpointed in research is the structure of the UK financial markets which places a premium on corporate control, so that UK firms are forced to pay higher dividends than their competitors abroad in order to resist the threat of takeover.[19]

The changes that have occurred in broadcasting in the 1980s and 1990s illustrate the problem. At the start of the 1980s the ITV companies had a narrow and, typically, privately controlled share ownership. But, since the Broadcasting Act of 1981, their share ownership has been widened and they are now traded on the stock exchange. The result has been a much sharper conflict than in the past between, on the one hand, the quasi-public service obligations placed on them first by the IBA and later by the ITC and, on the other hand, the need to generate cash flow and to increase dividends. Moreover, the battles within Granada which culminated in the sacking of David Plowright in February 1992 illustrate the extent to which the cash may sometimes be required not for investment in broadcasting, but to support the parent company.

Sustaining good quality broadcasting therefore faces a number of sharply conflicting concerns which it is difficult to meet simultaneously within a purely commercial structure. The economies of scale and scope which characterise much of the industry produce strong pressures towards concentration. Such concentration is desirable to the extent that it produces the profits to finance investment, and because it allows firms to capture some of the benefits of their own investment. In a democratic society undue concentration of media ownership is, however, highly undesirable. There therefore have to be cross-ownership rules to restrict it. Yet, if the threat of takeover is *permanently*, or near permanently, removed, and no other competitive pressure is put in its place, then there is nothing to keep the big commercial broadcasters on their toes.

In the past these conflicting considerations have been reconciled, at least to some extent, by the existence of the BBC. Being large, it has been able to carry out much of the R & D and, being driven by non-commercial considerations, it has been willing to see the results of the R & D disseminated to the commercial sector. Not that the situation was perfect. The 'comfortable duopoly' of the BBC and ITV was almost

---

15. Department of Trade and Industry (1990).

16. See NEDC (1983), Mowery (1986), and Cox and Kreigbaum (1989).

17. See Greenhalgh (1989).

18. See Finegold and Soskice (1988).

19. See Mayer and Alexander (1990).

certainly too comfortable in some respects. In the past the BBC has spent heavily on engineering technology, but not always to good effect (some of the major break-throughs came from the commercial sector). There may also have been an element of keeping production standards artificially high to make entry by competitors more difficult.[20]

Nevertheless, there is little doubt that, on balance, the system has worked rather well. In particular the BBC has been willing and able to take risks with programmes which purely commercial producers would probably have avoided and, in so doing, have helped the commercial sector to expand its range of programmes.[21] "Black Adder", for example, was not popular on its first showing and few people would have predicted the extensive appeal of the "Antiques Road Show".

Since 1982 the operation of the system has been further helped by the existence of Channel 4. Here, too, explicit public service obligations together with guaranteed income for several years has allowed C4 to take a longer term view than the market would allow. This room for manouevre, plus a remit which explicitly requires the channel to innovate and to provide programmes calculated to appeal to tastes and interests not generally catered for by ITV, has again extended consumers tastes in ways that many denied were possible in advance. For example, few people expected *Brookside* (which presented the city of Liverpool on network television for the first time) to be highly successful. In addition, the requirement that Channel 4 should buy all of its programmes from independent producers has been a useful incentive both to artistic innovation and to tighter control of costs (both in C4 and in the BBC).

Last but not least, the influence of the BBC has been especially beneficial in training where it has acted as a "talent-conveyor" belt, attracting many of the best staff early in their careers, training them well and then allowing the benefits of this training to spread throughout the broadcasting industry. In other words the "externality" problem in this area has been largely solved. Thus, even if the past system has been too uncompetitive in some respects, any move to a totally commercial system could well lead to market failures that would be more significant in the longer run.

Market Failure:
The Interaction of Consumption and Production

The possibility of a purely commercial broadcasting market failing to provide what individuals in society ultimately want is still more worrying when the interaction of the production with consumption is considered. It has been suggested above that in a pure market system consumers will fragment more than they really wish, will buy less good programmes than is collectively desirable and that individual consumers may under-invest in their own long term development because the beneficial effects

---

20. For further discussion of the 'comfortable duopoly' see Peacock (1986), chapter 4.

21. Katz and Ordover (1990) show how a purely private market will under invest in innovation that has complementary effects on competitors.

are only recognised in retrospect. It has also been argued that private sector broadcasters are likely to take too short a view, under-investing in training and in the production of good programmes.

Given these undesirable effects it is easy to imagine further adverse feedback effects. If consumers fragment and prove unwilling to pay the higher prices that good programmes will then require because they are unaware at the time either of the longer term benefits to themselves or to society, then broadcasters will not have the incentive to invest in producing such programmes. Conversely, if broadcasters are not providing good programmes, even well informed and far sighted consumers cannot buy them. To this may be added the possible external effects from one broadcaster to another via the consumer: each broadcaster may well consider his own (good) programme not commercially worthwhile unless other broadcasters are also transmitting good programmes that are gradually extending consumers' tastes.[22] Putting it bluntly, we will be "dumbed down" as the Americans say.

These theoretical concerns find support in practice both from experience abroad and from the history of broadcasting in the UK. Admittedly, there is, as yet, little *direct* evidence on exactly how a fully commercial system based largely on pay-TV would operate as no country has such a system. Even those with pay TV and dominated by commercial sectors gain by far the greatest part of their revenue from advertising. Nevertheless, the inferences that can be drawn are not encouraging. Other countries with a low element of public service broadcasting typically display poor quality, concentration of ownership plus frequent battles over ownership, flouting of regulators' rules and more or less subtle forms of government interference.

In France, for example, Canal Plus was launched in November 1984 as a subscription channel, but only six months later it was in financial trouble and so was allowed to accept advertising, and "Its major shareholder is the state-owned advertising company Havas, whose chairman ... has been a close friend and associate of Francois Mitterrand since 1950."[23] Although Canal Plus later became profitable, La Cinq, launched in 1986, filed for bankruptcy on New Year's Eve 1992 – and this in spite of offering quality news at one end and late night soft porn at the other plus financial support from Silvio Berlusconi. Moreover, with four new channels opened since 1984 it was found that "Between 1983 and 1988 the number of game shows screened jumped from four or five to fifteen or sixteen a week, ... the amount of light entertainment doubled [and] the number of feature films quadrupled".[24] The Financial Times described the effects of deregulation on French television as having heralded "an anarchic scenario of dozens of different channels pumping out soft porn and pulp programming punctuated by virtually unrestricted advertising".[25]

Experience in Germany and Italy offers similar warnings. German pay-TV appears to contain large amounts of pornography. In Italy, on the face of it there is

The Situation/result of commercial television in France

---

22. See Katz and Ordover (1990).

23. Forbes (1989), p.29.

24. Forbes (1989), p.33.

25. *Financial Times*, 27 December, 1991.

intense competition with well over 30 local channels, but, in practice, they are virtually all controlled by Fininvest, owned by Silvio Berlusconi, and the Fininvest channels have been much criticised for their down-market programming (consisting of some 90 per cent of entertainment and with over 50 per cent of total programming imported from the USA).

The case of the USA is the most interesting as it has the most commercial broadcasting in the world (though its enormous market makes it not directly comparable to European broadcasting). Here the move from a system with a small number of channels almost all financed by advertising to a multiplicity of channels and an expansion of pay-TV (both subscription and per programme) has genuinely extended choice. It has increased diversity, provided more and better news coverage and extended significantly the range of sports, music, language, educational, weather, travel and other special interest channels.[26] This is what one would expect. Advertising inevitably concentrates on the mass, middle income, market. Audience size, not how much the audience values the programme, is what matters. In addition, as channels multiply the incentive to look at minority interests rises . When there are only two channels they will each locate near the middle of the market and try to acquire fifty one per cent of it, whereas when there are, say, ten channels it becomes worthwhile to focus on a group that only constitutes ten per cent of the population. Television financed by pay per view is therefore far better than television financed by advertising at reflecting consumer wants.

Such observations, showing an improvement over time within the USA, are not, however, at odds with the argument above that a purely market driven system will fail in important ways. While the USA market undoubtedly offers considerable choice few would say that it offers television of such high quality as that of the UK, Australia or Canada, where there has been a much stronger contribution by PSBs. "Dumbing down", to use that USA term again, seems frequently to be the only concern.

We must also remember that the USA is a special situation. As a result of its vast market it faces less of a problem from the higher unit costs that accompany a proliferation of channels. In the USA channels can increase and yet the audience size per channel can still be high, so the trade-off between choice and quality is less severe that it will be for countries with smaller audiences. Moreover, even with such a large market it has only relatively recently begun to develop its own significant original productions for the cable channels and its public service broadcasting (reaching only about three per cent of the audience) have had to rely heavily in the past on importing programmes made abroad (especially from the UK).

More serious is that the USA provides little good broadcasting for children and what there is relies on advertising, or, worse still, on *insidious* advertising either via "infomercials" or by producing shows based on a toy (e.g. "Care Bears", "He Man", "Transformers", "GoBots" and "Masters of the Universe").[27] As Noam comments, "The most successful channel for children is Viacom's Nickelodeon, which has

---

26. Noam (1995).

27. Noam (1995) p.408 and 409.

30 percent of the viewing time of 6-11 year olds .... its programmes are more entertaining than educational." The USA is also thought to have provided only a "continuing narrow scope for political information".[28]

UK experience, in contrast, with a strong public service presence and ethos is widely acknowledged to have much good quality broadcasting and to have raised the quality over time. In his study of broadcasting in the 1980s Tim Madge refers to the extent to which the television programme-makers have enhanced the sophistication of their audiences so that "... programmes are made which simply could not have been "read" correctly a few years ago."[29]

Of course the current high quality of British television is partly the result of extremely good ITV programmes (three programmes often quoted in the 1980s as examples of high quality – "Brideshead Revisited", "The Jewel in the Crown" and "The South Bank Show" – were all broadcast on ITV). However, the context is crucial. As "... ITV executives admit, without the BBC as a constant reminder – and threat to their audiences – the best ITV programmes would be rarely made. Producers in commercial television unashamedly use the BBC to argue their case for the equivalent of public service programming."[30]

The Company You Keep[31]

These points about quality can be made another way. In many aspects of our lives we readily recognise that the environment within which we live and the people with whom we work can have an enormous influence on what we do, or do not, achieve. To take just a few examples: everyone wants children to go to high quality schools, or sports people to have the best coaches, or firms to learn from best practice worldwide. Yet is not television part of the company we all keep? On average, people watch it for no less than 25 hours per week. Including radio, the BBC estimate that the average household spends more than a quarter of all their leisure time watching or listening to the BBC. Moreover, children watch it more than the average. So also do households with children. It is impossible to measure what effects this has since it is not possible to run the experiment of what society without television would be like. Nevertheless it is inconceivable that it has anything other than a powerful effect.

As Robyn Williams, Australia's foremost producer of popular science programmes, comments when discussing the effects of downmarket broadcasting, "Of course the Popzonk/Newzak/Blisscomb culture need not go hand in hand with a world marooned somewhere in Mad Max country. But somehow I see them together. It is likely that the broadcasting (the *communication*) system we choose for our future world will come wedded to certain social values, demonstrating, perhaps, what kinds of communities we want to enjoy in the next century."[32]

---

28. Lange and Woldt (1995) p.484.

29. Madge (1989) p.59.

30. Madge (1989) p.209.

31. I owe this felicitous concept to Danny Quah.

32. Williams (1996) p.15.

A more specific example of the importance of "the company you keep" is the imaginative, creative and lively character of much UK TV advertising. Being sandwiched between programmes that are themselves, in general, well made and imaginative is undoubtedly part of the reason. The advertisers have been put on their toes and have responded – and, no doubt, some of the effects also run the other way. The important point is that each has stretched the other and so each has achieved more – and this has not been a pure market outcome.

V   Citizenship, Culture and Community

T he argument, so far, has been that there is a case for public service broadcasting so as to make good the deficiencies of the market in providing what well informed *consumers*, acting either individually or in aggregate, would wish to buy over the longer term. A quite separate argument arises from the fact that there are parts of our lives to which the market is simply not relevant. To be more concrete, we watch television and listen to the radio, not just as consumers, but also as *citizens*.

Our citizenship carries with it three separate implications. First, as citizens we have rights. This includes the right to certain core information about our own society. Thus almost everyone would agree that anyone is entitled to know *without having to pay for it* such basic things as the key items of news, their legal rights, who their MP is, etc. It is immediately obvious that the market makes no provision for this (any more than it does for basic education or primary health care for the poor). Moreover there is a danger that, in the absence of appropriate public policy, the new technology of the Internet and Intranets (closed networks using Internet technology) will create a world in which on the one side there is high quality commercially provided information and on the other side, in the public domain, only poor quality information.[33] In this new context the informational role of a public service broadcaster operating universally is therefore more important than ever. As the local public library declines, so the ever present public broadcaster must fill the gap – and for zero charge at the margin.

Second, as citizens we have views about society that cannot be captured just in our buying and selling. In particular in a wide ranging investigation carried out in 1994 and 1995 the Bertelsmann Foundation working with the European Institute for the Media found that in all ten countries covered people expected and wanted "socially responsible television".[34] Moreover they concluded that "responsibility in programming has a chance only if and when it has been defined and constantly pursued as a strategic aim in the management [of the broadcaster]".[35] It is difficult to see how both profitability and responsibility can be constant strategic aims at the same time. In the competitive market place profitability is bound to take priority.

Third, as citizens we are members of a community. It has been said that while we are all individual we are also all individual *somebodies*. In other words our sense of our own identity derives from how we see ourselves in relation to society and from where we 'locate' ourselves within it. Stated simply, there is intrinsic value to

---

33. Graham (1995 and 1996).
34. Bertelsmann (1995) p.463.
35. Bertelsmann (1995) p.6.

individuals if they have a sense of community – to be alienated is literally to lose a part of oneself.

The crucial importance of broadcasting in this context is that for the great majority of people it is today their major source of information about the world, beyond that of family, friends and acquaintances. Television provides not only the hard facts, but also the fuzzy categories – the social, ethnic, psychological, etc., concepts within which we must make sense of the world. It also supplies a set of fantasies, emotions and fictional images with which we construct our understanding (or misunderstanding) of all those parts of society beyond our immediate surroundings. It is therefore part not just of how we see ourselves in relation to the community, or communities, within which we are embedded, but also part of how we understand the community – indeed part of where the very idea of community arises and is given meaning.

The general importance of community and of a common culture to the well-being of a society and its citizens is widely-recognized.[36] Culture and community provide a common frame of reference in terms of which to comprehend the history, present and future of one's society and of one's own place within it, and so to make sense of the decisions one has to take both as an individual and as a citizen. Moreover, the texts, practices and traditions which make it up function as sources of aesthetic and moral understanding and empowerment, as well as providing a focus for communal identification.

There is little doubt that in today's society the viewing of television is part of what creates any sense of commonality that we may have. This is true as much of low as of high culture. The latest episode of a soap opera or a recent football match can function as a topic upon which all members of the society can form an opinion or converse with one another regardless of the differences in their life-style, social class or status group. Given that any society must embody such socio-cultural differences, the value of a community where people have things in common and can interact on that basis is or should be obvious.

The value of commonality, the value of shared experience, the value of self-identity and the value provided by non-stereotypical portrayal of other cultures are not considerations that do, or could, enter into the transactions of the market place – but they are values nonetheless. For all of these reasons there is a case for a public service broadcaster, one of whose objectives would be the provision of those broadcasts which we are entitled to as citizens. Moreover, a genuinely national public service broadcaster could provide the material for such commonality in ways that other broadcasting organisations, with a less extensive and penetrating reach, could not match.

---

36. Except, that is, by some economists who have read Adam Smith's *Wealth of Nations*, but who have failed to realise how much Smith's view of the market depended on the social context described in his earlier work, *The Theory of Moral Sentiments*.

Fragmentation

This general point about commonality takes on added importance as well as a different form in the context of a pluralist society, such as Britain in the late 1990s. As the processes of technological, economic and social change increase in rapidity, traditional forms of social unity can break down and new sub-cultures based on partially overlapping but less widely-shared and equally deep commitments to certain forms or styles of life (ones based on class, region, religion, race, sexual orientation and so on) can proliferate. To this must be added the near certainty that a "free market" in broadcasting based on an abundance of channels would itself fragment audiences and, by so doing, increase the sense of separateness. In such a context, the risks of socio-cultural fragmentation are high, and so is the value of any medium by means of which that fragmentation could be combatted.

As technology fragments the market, it is therefore entirely appropriate for public service broadcasting in 1990s Britain to contribute towards the (re)construction and maintenance of a common national culture – not a single dominant culture, but a set of shared values that are accommodating enough to accept on equal terms as many as possible of the minority group cultures that go to make up such a pluralist society, and thereby minimise its tendency towards fragmentation. What would be shared by the members of such a culture would *not* be belief in a particular form of life, but rather an understanding of the lives of other citizens, together with a shared acknowledgement of their worth or validity. And it is this latter requirement which specifies the sense in which the various sub-cultures are accepted within (form part of) a common culture on equal terms with one another.

The importance of a public service broadcaster in this process would be that by broadcasting informed and accurate representations of minority cultures, it would help to maintain the culture's shared emphasis upon respect for human life – it would do so by disseminating the knowledge that forms the essential basis for acknowledging those aspects of the minority cultures which make them worthy of respect. Moreover, the extent and penetration of a national broadcaster would be both a requirement and a significant advantage; for in modern society, the key way of ensuring the legitimation of a given sub-culture by conferring a public profile upon it is through television.

One final area under the heading of citizenship and community where a public service broadcaster should be expected to play a special role is in the broadcasting of National Events. Here, the idea would be that a public service broadcaster should be given the responsibility to broadcast events which, going beyond questions of purely sub-culture-specific interests, are of genuinely national interest. The events in question would include happenings anywhere in the world that are of significance to virtually anyone (eg the collapse of the Berlin Wall) or to this country in particular (eg the UK athletics team in the Olympic Games), as well as events in the UK that are primarily of importance to its citizens (eg the resignation of a Prime Minister, Royal weddings or European and General Elections). Such a broadcasting service would help to maintain a sense of national identity which transcends more local communal identifications and allows individuals to understand themselves as members of a particular nation. And a public service broadcaster's relative advantage here would derive from its experience and expertise at performing such functions, together with its capacity for genuinely national dissemination.

VI Democracy and the Mass Media

It is a basic principle of a democratic society that votes should not be bought and sold. This alone is sufficient justification for broadcasting not being entirely commercial. It is, by the same token, the major reason why broadcasting should not be directly under the control of the State. There has to be a source of information which can be trusted to be accurate in its news, documentaries and current affairs programmes and to be impartial between different social and political views. It is a necessary, but not sufficient condition, for this to be possible that some at least of the broadcasters be independent of any political party and of any business interest.

In the late 1990s there are good grounds for thinking that the need for a public service broadcaster to exist and to uphold the principles of truth and impartiality will be even greater than in the past. Two factors in particular stand out. First, the pluralism that characterises today's Britain, together with the very speed and extent of social change which makes information so vital, have ensured that many traditional networks for the dissemination of information (ranging from the extended family through the close-knit neighbourhood to stable, apprenticeship-based workplaces) have disappeared or been severely weakened. Second, there will soon be many more purveyors of information – of hard news, soft news, of fact and of faction.

It is not enough, however, for truth to be upheld. It must also be available – and available to all. The advantages of the BBC (and to a similar but lesser extent, C4) in these circumstances as important alternative networks are manifold. It has national scope and is easily accessible; its tradition of dedicated public service together with its world wide reputation provides the basis for trust without which much information is just propaganda; and its independence from both Government and commercial or market-place pressures should make it more capable of representing unpopular or otherwise unpalatable truths. These arguments are not, however, absolute ones, but contingent upon the behaviour of the BBC. While the BBC's reputation is mostly deserved, there have been times when it has been justifiably criticised for being too much under the influence of the Government. Moreover, a number of supposedly "public service" broadcasters in other countries have been little more than mouthpieces for the State. It follows that the reputation of the BBC has to continue to be *earned*.

A closely related point is that, in general, broadcasting in the UK has been responsible and not corrupt. The particular structure of UK broadcasting which has managed – at least until recently – to put the broadcasters in a position where they do not depend from day to day on immediate financial pressures from either the market or the State has undoubtedly helped. Thus all the terrestrial broadcasters have carried programmes such as *Panorama*, *World in Action* and *The Cook Report* which have been willing to criticise vested interests and to expose corruption.

Whether such strong investigative journalism will persist in the commercial sector in the future is, however, less clear. In the past the IBA took responsibility for the programme content, but since the Broadcasting Act 1990 and the "lighter touch" regulation of the ITC, the programme makers are responsible for content. The result may well be greater caution on the part of the separate companies (and within on the part of individual journalists). If so, the need for the BBC to continue in this area is all the greater.[37]

It should also not be assumed (as it often is) that commercial broadcasting is necessarily *freer* of politics than public service broadcasting just because one is public and one is commercial. In France the close connection between Canal Plus and Mitterrand has already been noted. In Italy the interventions have been far more blatant. In the March 1994 elections Berlusconi used his three TV stations reaching 40 per cent of the Italian audience to give unremitting support to his own political party, Forza Italia, and the wider grouping of the Freedom Alliance. Subsequent research showed not only that there was a bigger swing to the right (3.5 per cent more) among Berlusconi viewers than the electorate in general, but also that this swing could not be explained by the fact that viewers of Berlusconi channels were *already* more right wing. Viewers of these channels were found to be middle of the road and only shifted their voting *after* watching the Berlusconi channels.[38] Then, of course, after the election, the Government was Berlusconi and in the referendum on whether Berlusconi should be obliged to sell off two of its three TV networks, Fininvest used its networks to support the Vote No campaign. Fininvest carried 520 spots for the Vote No campaign as compared with only 42 for the Vote Yes campaign which was effectively forced off the air because its slots were placed in such disadvantageous positions.[39]

Common Knowledge[40]

So far the arguments about the relationship between the mass media and democracy strongly reinforce the case for public service broadcasters existing as major sources of independent, accurate and impartial information. However, the ideas of accurate information and of impartiality need to be seen in a wider context. Although it is not often recognised society depends critically on the existence of "common knowledge" – what everybody knows that everybody knows. Most of the time the existence of such knowledge is taken for granted. However, it plays a role in society that is both more profound and more important than at first it seems.

The influence of common knowledge is more profound than it might seem because *any* debate requires *some* common knowledge – as a minimum, it has to be agreed what is being debated. Moreover, in modern societies the media is one major way in which common knowledge is *created*. It is also more important than it might seem because almost all solutions to problems require the *extension* of common knowledge. In order to be *agreed*, solutions have to be based on a common understanding of the situation. Common knowledge is therefore a *pre-condition* of many coordination problems in democratic societies.

---

37. I am grateful to Jocelyn Hay for this point.

38. Gallucci (1994)

39. "One voice on Italy TV" *Free Press*, July/August 1995

40. In economics "common knowledge" is a technical term in the theory of games meaning what is known by all and is true. We use it here to cover a broader category of cases.

Agreeing on solutions and agreeing on *correct* solutions are not, however, the same thing. Or to put the same point another way, knowledge, which implies that what is known is true, is not the same as belief, which may or may not be true. The "power of the witchdoctor" may have been thought of as common knowledge, but strictly speaking it was only "common belief". Another more contemporary example which displays both the power of the media and the danger and inefficiency of inaccurate 'common knowledge' , if we may use that contradiction, comes from the experience reported by the Labour MP, Dianne Abbott. When visiting a London school she asked what number the pupils would dial in an emergency. The answer from many was "911" – the US emergency number!

This example also illustrates that "knowledge" and "information" need to be understood as including much more than is dealt with by news programmes. It also covers the discussions of news, trends and images that are to be found on radio phone-in shows, chat shows, That's Life and so on, as well as the scientific and cultural matters typically dealt with by programmes such as Horizon and Arena, not to mention the life-styles presented in so many contemporary fictional creations.

Furthermore, central to the idea of the democratic society is that of the well-informed and self-determining individual; but, if individuals are to be genuinely autonomous, it is not sufficient for them merely to receive information (no matter how much and how impartially presented), they must be able to *understand* it. They must be able to make sense of it in ways that relate to their own lives and decisions. Neither facts on the one hand nor opinions on the other (although both are important) are sufficient; for neither are utilisable by those who absorb them unless they are made the subject of reasoned analysis – unless, in other words, they are not merely transmitted but presented (organised, submitted to informed and coherent criticism from as many perspectives as possible) in a way which allows them to be understood and thereby incorporated into the audience's own judgements. Information without 'organising insights' is just noise.

The media has therefore a double responsibility. First, programmes need to handle information in such a way that it increases understanding and creates knowledge. Second, programmes need to ensure, as far as possible, that such knowledge correctly represents the world as we know it.

It is worth noting here the sharp contrast between the generally responsible attitude of talk show hosts in the UK and those in some other countries. In April 1996 the New York radio station WABC fired a talk show host called Bob Grant, but this was only after twenty-five years of regular attacks on blacks, Hispanics and other minorities. An ABC producer who was asked whether Bob Grant's remarks were an example of free speech that should be protected under the First Amendment or whether they were verbal pollution replied, "If the person has good ratings a station has to overlook the garbage that he spews out". The same producer added, "[In the USA] radio is the only serious soapbox the racists have. Our advertisers are aware that hate sells their products".[41]

41. Quoted in Williams (1996).

33

The editorial responsibility that is so obviously lacking in this case is not surprising. If the product sells and makes a profit that is all that is required. Ethical judgements, even where the only ethical requirement is a respect for evidence, is not part of its natural domain. Its *purpose* is to make money, not to sustain democracy, nor to expand common knowledge nor to extend the tastes and capacities of its audience.

Purposes matter. Almost all societies allow children to attend a single school for many years. The school is therefore the monopoly provider of both information and understanding – and at a particularly formative stage in a person's life. Yet an equivalent commercial monopoly, even later in life, is strongly resisted. The reason is that schools and commerce have different objectives. The *purpose* of a school is not to indoctrinate, but to educate. Indeed the exception proves the rule. In the rare number of cases when people do object to the influence of schools it is usually because the school is suspected of peddling a particular point of view to the detriment of education.

Closely related to this is what can be described as the "Yes, Minister" problem. Someone has a piece of information. You may know that they have it and you may know that the information would be useful to you. However, you may not know what question to ask to elucidate that information. As the "Yes, Minister" programme brought out so well, some civil servants like being in that kind of position, because information is power and power is not always given up easily. Typically the way in which this problem has been handled in the past has been through education. The *purpose* of educators is to empower other people and they want to teach people what questions to ask and how to use information to understand the world. Such an assumption cannot be made of the commercial world. The purpose of the commercial world is to make a profit. Nothing wrong in that, but it is different.

In brief, if democracy and the role of its citizens is left just to the market, they will be poorly served. There will be a gap in broadcasting which in a fully functioning democracy requires public service broadcasting to fill it. Moreover one key principle for public service broadcasters to follow on this count is that they should aim to extend the understanding and experience of those who watch or listen. It is important to emphasise that this core principle is not restricted in its application to certain types of current affairs or documentary programming (although of course it does apply to them). Drama, soap operas, chat shows, children's programmes and situation comedies could all contribute to empowering as large a body of the citizenry as possible.

Public service broadcasters performing this function would therefore provide a central forum – the public space – within which society could engage in the process of extending its common knowledge as well as in illuminating and either re-affirming, questioning or extending its already-existing values.

VII   Industrial Policy

One final argument against relying entirely on the market remains. The countries which have performed best at producing programmes the rest of the world wants to see and hear have not been those dominated either by commercial broadcasting or by state run broadcasting, but those in which there has been a powerful public service tradition (suitably distanced from Government) combined with a commercial sector. The UK and to a lesser extent Australia are the two prime examples. The USA has, of course, been dominant in the audio-visual industry, but this has been because of its power in films (derived from the dominance of Hollywood), *not* because of its television or radio. Equally few would look to Italy or France where state influence in broadcasting has been far too excessive to allow creative ideas to flourish.

The UK's success has been led by the BBC and is the result of extensive investment in talent over many years. The result is that the BBC has developed a *comparative advantage*. No amount of abstract theorising justifies throwing success away. It would be even more foolish to duplicate (or to try to duplicate) in other broadcasting organisations identical strengths to those that the BBC already possesses – the attempt would probably damage both the old and the new (the remit for Channel 4 carefully avoided making this mistake).

Many of the areas in which the BBC probably has a comparative advantage have, of course, emerged purely contingently through historical commitments. For example, the BBC has long standing connections with specific events and areas of programming (e.g. the Proms, Wimbledon, coronations, music, sport, nature programmes, news and current affairs). In some of these areas it is likely that through the process of "learning by doing" the BBC has developed genuine advantages quite irrespective of its particular concerns as a public service broadcaster. Where the BBC has such an advantage, but only where it has such advantage, the accumulated experience, expertise, economies of scale and intimacy with the relevant organisational bodies should be capitalised upon, not ignored nor regarded as optional.

Of course there is a danger that this argument could be misused, being deployed as a defence of everything that the BBC now does, but this is not the intention at all. The point is a simple one. Activities that the market might support should not be stripped away from the BBC just because it is a public broadcaster. Equally, activities that the market might handle better should not be left with the BBC just because they have been with the BBC in the past. The decision should be pragmatic not ideological.

VIII   Rules-Based Intervention v Public Service Broadcasting

The arguments above provide a strong case for thinking that broadcasting should not be left just to the market. There is therefore a *prima facie* case for intervention, but such arguments provide no guidance on the *form* that intervention should take. Why, one has to ask, could market failures not be dealt with by regulation as occurs, for example, in the case of health and safety legislation? Moreover, there are two reasons why this question is particularly pertinent (especially in the UK). First, in the UK the regulation of the commercial sector, through, first, the IBA and later the ITC, is thought by many to have worked rather well in the past. Second, and more fundamentally, almost no-one maintains that broadcasting should be wholly unregulated.

Our answer to this question is in two parts. First, we agree that in some cases regulation *is* appropriate. For example, if the *only* concern of public policy was that child pornography should not be broadcast then rules banning this activity could make an important contribution. The same is true of concentration. If the goal is to stop a single person or organisation controlling large part of the media then laws limiting cross-ownership of media outlets have an important role to play.

However, our second answer is far more important. We consider that in the particular case of broadcasting, rules-based intervention is necessary but *not* sufficient, especially not in the new environment of the 1990s.

The first reason why rules are insufficient is that many of the issues concerning broadcasting are qualitative rather than quantitative in nature. This is self-evidently true of quality itself, but it applies equally to the discussion above of the importance of maintaining a sense of community as well as valuing a democratic society. These broad principles which should guide part of broadcasting could not be incorporated in any *precise* set of rules – indeed it is the impossibility of doing so that differentiates qualitative from quantitative assessments.[42]

Of course, it would still be possible for there to be a legislative framework containing these principles and for the *judgements* about the principles to be delegated to a broadcasting authority (as used to be done for the IBA). However, once rules are discretionary, a new set of issues arises. The regulators, unable to appeal to a firm rule, may give in to pressure from those they are regulating. If so, the apparent attraction of rules-based intervention is much diminished. Similarly, if producers are required to act in necessarily loosely defined ways and in ways that are *against* their commercial interests, it may be more efficient to establish a public body with explicitly non-commercial goals than to police a complex and imprecise set of regulations.

---

42. Some of the problems of regulating public utilities where there is an element of quality are discussed in Rovizzi and Thompson (1991). However, they frequently mean not "quality", but "standards" and therefore treat quality as quantifiable – a confusion which the English language has been designed to avoid!

The second reason why rules are insufficient is that rules are, at best, negative – especially when regulating *against* strong commercial forces. While regulation may, therefore, be able to protect standards, for example by *preventing* the display of excessive violence or sexual material considered offensive, it is much less well suited to *promoting* quality. This point is central. At numerous points in the earlier argument we have shown that *purposes* matter. But purposes are about *doing* things – educating, informing and entertaining, for example. Such purposes cannot possibly be achieved by rules because rules cannot make things happen. This is of great importance because, in the case of broadcasting we have shown that there are gaps in the system which require *positive* pressure to correct them. This is why, corresponding to each area in which the market would fall down, it has been possible above to identify one or more primary *objectives* that a public service broadcaster should pursue. To offset market failure it should aim to expand quality and to extend individuals ideas of what they can achieve; to meet the requirements of citizenship it should provide for the needs of community (or communities); to sustain democracy it should extend common knowledge and empower those that watch it or listen to it; and in industrial policy PSBs should concentrate on those areas in which they have already established a comparative advantage.

Moreover, none of these objectives is genre specific. Neither enrichment, nor our ideas of community, nor common knowledge, nor comparative advantage are restricted to some 'high-brow' ghetto. What will matter most of the time is not *what kind* of programmes are made, but *how* they are made – hardly the task for a regulator.

Nevertheless, at the risk of repetition, is should be emphasised that the structure of broadcasting envisaged here would include some regulation. Indeed one fundamental point of this section is that, in the particular case of broadcasting, regulation and direct public provision can be and should be complementary to one another. Equally important is that the particular mix of regulation and public provision should change as the context changes.

In the late 1990s there are two reasons why this context is altering in ways that make rules-based intervention less effective. First, there is technical change. At the moment the Government retains the ability to allocate frequencies and so regulation can be enforced. However, as satellite broadcasting becomes more widespread such regulation becomes more difficult. For example, within Europe there will be a number of satellite broadcasters each of which is aiming primarily at a single country, but whose signal can be received in a number of surrounding countries. If so, which countries' regulations apply? And how is the "external" broadcaster to be forced to comply with two sets of possibly incompatible regulations? The answer to such problems is not to conclude that regulation is impossible, but to reconsider the objectives and to see whether there is some other way of influencing the market. One obvious possibility is to use public service broadcasting. If so, public service broadcasting will become more, rather than less, important as the technology develops.

Second, there is the new commercial climate. As noted earlier, the ITV companies are now traded on the stock exchange. They are also operating under the new franchise system. Both of these developments have increased the pressure to maximise profits and, frequently, short run profits at that. This is a marked change from the position in the 1960s and 1970s when the system had a degree of slack in it which allowed the private companies to strike a balance between, on the one hand, their commercial concerns and, on the other hand, the public service obligations placed upon them by the legislation. In short, any purely regulatory system will be operating under far more strain than in the past.

One particular area in which this will be important will be research and development. We noted earlier the way in which the existence of the BBC has eased the policy conflict that exists in this area (if private sector R&D is protected by strong patents it will under disseminate the results of research, but, if it is not protected by strong patents, it will under invest in research). The greater the competition the greater this conflict becomes (since competition pushes down prices and profits and so reduces the ability to finance investment). In effect intense competition makes firms focus more and more on the short term. In these circumstances the case for the BBC carrying out some of the R&D for the broadcasting industry is therefore increased.

Closely related to this is need to maintain training. It is well known that where there is a multiplicity of small firms will frequently "free ride", each of them not doing enough of it because, once an employee moves, the benefits of that person's training are lost to that firm. Moreover, the tendency to act in this way is greater the more intense is the competition – firms just cannot afford to invest in benefits which they do not capture. The 'casualisation' of production is therefore not conducive to the development of skills. Of course there need to be independent programme makers – there is no presumption here that the BBC should produce everything in-house – but, as noted earlier, the "conveyor belt" of training provided by the BBC helps to solve the externality problem in this area. And, given more competition elsewhere in the system, the case for the "conveyor belt" is greater not less. In addition to helping the broadcasting sector directly through its own training, the presence of the BBC probably helps in a further way. The independents are likely to keep up their training by more than would otherwise be the case because they face, in the form of the BBC, a moderately regular and reliable outlet – and an outlet that wants to buy quality programmes.

In the late 1990s both the globalisation of broadcasting and the greater intensity of competition would therefore be reasons why trying to influence the market through the presence of a public service broadcaster would become more rather than less relevant. However, if such a public service broadcaster is to exist there has to be some stability of the institutional framework in order to maintain and extend standards and practices. Moreover, the "conveyor belt"of training made possible by the BBC provides a culture of quality and a commitment to the ideals of public service broadcasting that should not be thrown away. It requires an institutional context to sustain it and it benefits the whole of broadcasting.

The inescapable conclusion of all these arguments is that there should be a 'centre of excellence', such as the BBC, which both makes and broadcasts programmes. It is possible that there could be more than one such centre (as it could be argued there is now with the BBC and, though in a different way, Channel 4), but the need for a critical mass suggests that at most there would be two or three such institutions rather than a series of independent producers. Three reasons in particular point in this direction:

(i)   In the conception of a public service broadcaster put forward here it must be large enough to influence the market. Without this it cannot act as the guarantor of quality. A series of separate *small* producers sustained by public money would be beside the point and, on their own, would have no influence whatsoever on the broadcasting by the commercial channels.

(ii)   Only an obviously *national* broadcaster would be able to generate the complex and rich sense of community that citizens have a right to expect in the pluralistic society of which the UK now consists.

(iii)   The trust and reputation that the BBC already has is an invaluable asset which should not be discarded. Moreover this reputation is attached to the institution as a whole not to individual programmes.

One final point about the role of a public service broadcaster remains to be underlined. Each of the first three grounds for public service broadcasting – the need to promote high quality broadcasting, the need to generate a sense of community and the need for citizens to have and understand the information essential for the functioning of democracy – exist independent of the particular set of choices made *now*.

Suppose, purely hypothetically, that everyone today had full information and full autonomy and that they chose a particular (narrow) mix of programmes. This outcome would then have occurred without market failure. Nevertheless, given the potential interdependence between the broadcasting on offer and the preferences of consumers, there would still remain the requirement that the *next* generation of consumers should be presented with a diverse, informative and enriching range of programmes so that *their* right to exercise *their* choice with full information and full autonomy would be ensured. The market, left to itself, would not guarantee this right. Consumers with their taste unexposed to, and underdeveloped by, a richer fare would not and could not demand programmes that did not exist and so producers, for their part, would experience no unfilled demand. There would be no driving force towards better quality.

Similarly, suppose, again hypothetically, that the interaction of today's consumers with the market produced a myriad of channels each with its own format, each differentiated (however marginally) from the others, presenting an endless stream of diverse information and diverse life-styles without apparent connection. Here again there would remain the case, many would say the imperative need, to present within one universally available channel the idea of a society (or societies) with which future generations of individuals could identify if they so wished. We cannot choose to belong to a society unless a society exists to which we may choose to belong. To deny future generations this would be to deny them a choice, not just between brand A and brand B, but about how they might wish to lead their lives and the kinds of people they might wish to become.

On all three grounds (quality, community and democracy), therefore, a major argument for public service broadcasting today is that it provides an insurance policy for the desires, needs and rights of the generations of tomorrow. Moreover, this is not an insurance policy that any form of rules-based intervention will provide. What is required, especially within the increasingly de-regulated environment of the late 1990s, is a public service broadcaster, widening and extending choice, both by its own existence and by its influence on other broadcasters.

There is much misunderstanding on this question of choice. It is clear that the fear of censorship and, in particular, of hidden censorship has loomed large in the minds of many of the critics of public service broadcasting and in attacks on the elitism and paternalism of the BBC in particular. Such fears and criticisms were understandable in the past when spectrum scarcity prevailed and when, as a result, access to televisual media was, as the critics would have said, exclusively under the control of either state funded or state authorised institutions. But this will not be the broadcasting world of the next century. Satellite, cable and video mean that private televisual media will expand considerably irrespective of the role played by public broadcasters and so, in this new world, provided only that the costs are met and the general law of the land is respected, no-one will be *denied* making or seeing anything they wish. On the contrary in the face of the new technology which threatens excessive fragmentation, the loss of common knowledge and low quality it will be the existence of a public service broadcaster which *widens choice* and which, through its commitment to provide understanding, gives the *means to make the choice for oneself.* Thus a vibrant commercial system *plus* a context influenced by public service broadcasting would be the very opposite of elitism, paternalism or censorship.

In other words, public production and public broadcasting is needed for the health of the *whole* system. Thus the BBC, or something very like it, is central, not an optional add-on. In short, such a public service broadcaster is a real public good and the true justification for public funding is not the 'financing the BBC', but the financing of the quality of the system.

Just as in the nineteenth century no-one thought that regulation could *provide* public libraries so in the twenty first century regulation cannot provide public service broadcasting. Public service broadcasting exists to meet goals that are not those of the market and no amount of regulation can make the market pursue such goals. Thus while the BBC has no *right* to exist, there are *purposes for its existence.*

IX What Form of Public Finance?

Other countries which operate public service broadcasting use a wide variety of types of finance. Many countries, including Japan, France, Germany, Italy, Denmark, Sweden, the Netherlands, Ireland and New Zealand have licence fees, whereas Australia, Canada and the USA have various forms of government grant. However, Canada supplements the government grant with advertising and the USA (with a very small public service element) relies partially on private donations, while France, Germany, Italy and Ireland combine licence fee revenue with advertising. Of these countries only the UK, Japan and Sweden (relying almost entirely on the licence fee) and Australia (now relying mainly on grant – they used to have a fee) have what might be described as "pure" systems.

The next two questions to be decided are therefore:-

a. Should the funding take the form of a direct grant from Government and thus be part of the annual programme of public expenditure or, as now, be provided through a licence fee or a hypothecated tax? And, in either case, should the public funding provide the whole revenue or should some come from the private sector?

b. If a special tax were appropriate, what form should it take?

These issues are discussed next. The questions of both the potential yield and the desirable yield are left until later.

Direct Grant or Special Tax?

Looking first at the comparison between "pure" systems, there are four considerations which suggest that public funding should *not* take the form of a direct grant from Government and thus be part of the annual programme of public expenditure.

First, there is the need for the institution to be seen to be, and to believe itself to be, at arm's length from the Government. This is a prerequisite for it sustaining a reputation for impartiality and for fearless reporting. Its independence from Government is just as important as its freedom from immediate commercial pressures. It is notable that Australia (relying on grants) is a country where the scale of funding has been increased or decreased – in recent years, mostly decreased – for political purposes.[43] Furthermore, there would be an ever present likelihood that the grant for the BBC would be squeezed in order to create room for extra spending in areas which were particularly pressing politically at the time.

Second, it is essential for any broadcaster's ability to maintain and extend quality that it be able to take a medium to long term view of its future plans. It must therefore be able to count on a reasonably predictable and reliable source of income over at least the next 3-5 years. Direct annual funding would not meet this.

---

43. See Harding (1985).

Third, the annual negotiations involved in direct funding not only create uncertainty, but absorb a significant amount of the time of senior managers which could be better devoted to running broadcasting.

Fourth, it is only with secure funding over a run of years that a public service broadcaster will be able to avoid the opposite temptation of starting to boost its income from commercial sources (as the BBC, faced with a squeeze on its public revenue, has recently begun to do with the formation of BBC Enterprises Ltd and BBC World Wide) and then finding itself, as a result, being faced with a confusion of purpose.

The last of these considerations is highly pertinent to the merits, or otherwise, of "mixed" public and private systems of finance. An organisation such as the BBC can either be asked to maximise its profits or it can be asked to maximise the effectiveness of its public service broadcasting. It *cannot*, however, sensibly be asked to serve two masters, attempting to maximise both simultaneously. Moreover, in the future when the industry will be more de-regulated the commercial pressures on the rest of the industry and thus also from the rest of the industry will be higher than in the past (when even ITV has been constrained by law to take account of public service obligations). In the new environment there will therefore be an *increased* need for the BBC to concentrate on its public service role and for it to be neither pulled by commercial considerations nor pushed by short term pressures of a different kind from government. These arguments suggest that it would be as much a mistake to go for "mixed" public and private finance as to go for a direct government grant.

The arguments so far lead to the conclusion that a successful public broadcaster, large enough to make a significant contribution to the totality of UK broadcasting output, must be primarily funded from sources which are not based on charges at the "point of sale" (because of the ways in which the market fails). The objections to advertising as a form of finance are more severe.[44] Once the BBC ventures down this path, it will almost certainly be forced to proceed further, until eventually it becomes indistinguishable from a commercial broadcaster. Indeed, any form of commercial finance, if it becomes too large, should be viewed with suspicion. This includes the development of income from "sponsorship", which may at first seem attractive, but in fact simply represents advertising in a more insidious form. So, if the UK is to have a successful public service broadcaster, we simply have to resort eventually to public finance.

---

44. One of the great and lasting benefits of the Peacock Report was that it showed the advertising route for BBC finance to be a treacherous cul-de-sac.

X   What Form of Special Tax?

Ideally, the form of finance for public service broadcasting should fulfil the following characteristics:

(i)   It should be related in some way to receipt of the service, so that consumers make a direct link between the benefits they receive, and the outlays they make. This maximises the likelihood that the charge will remain politically acceptable.

(ii)   It should be at a flat rate so that there is a direct link between the level of the service received by everyone, and the level of the charge made on everyone.[45]

(iii)   There should ideally be some form of income-elasticity in receipts from the charge, so that they grow at least in line with nominal GDP (i.e. the growth in the receipts should cover both economy-wide inflation, and should contain an element of real growth for the increased provision of services in an expanding economy).

(iv)   As noted above, the setting of the charge should be subject to minimum interference from the government of the day.

(v)   The charge should be relatively easy to collect, enforce and administer.

Although the licence fee has been widely criticised in the past, and although it no longer fulfils the third of the above requirements now that the move from black and white to colour television has reached its natural limitations, it is doubtful whether there is a form of public finance which is likely to prove generally superior – though a number of alternatives that have been suggested are discussed below. If the licence fee continues, therefore, to be the best form of public funding available, and, if the licence fee has to be set at a level that gives a public service broadcaster a significant influence on the broadcasting market, it is necessary to look at what has been happening to this source of revenue in the recent past and at how it might grow (or decline) on a variety of assumptions about the future. To this we now turn.

---

45. This makes the charge regressive in its distributive effects, but this might be acceptable provided that the charge can be kept fairly low. In addition there is no good reason for exempting particular categories of consumers from paying the charge.

XI   The History of the Licence Fee

The BBC licence fee is something of an anomaly in the history of British public finance. Very few of Britain's public services have in the past been financed by fixed rate levies. Most have been financed either from general taxation (like the National Health Service) or from charges on the end user (like public transport), with the latter often being topped up by subsidies coming from general taxation. However, the licence fee is not unique – until privatisation, domestic water charges were levied at a fixed rate for all houses attached to the mains water supply. The licence fee operates on the same principle – all homes equipped with at least one colour television are expected to make a flat rate contribution to the cost of providing the BBC's services.

Whatever the arguments about the merits of the licence fee, there is no questioning its longevity. It was first introduced for radio in 1922, and it has formed the basis for the financing of the BBC ever since. Many times, governments have seriously considered replacing it, but they have always been driven back to the status quo. Even in the changing circumstances of the 1990s, so far this has continued to happen. Apart from the manifest problems with all the suggested alternatives to the licence fee, politicians of all parties have been influenced by the fact that, unlike almost all other taxes, it is not particularly unpopular with the electorate. Most voters seem able to connect the payment of the licence fee directly to the receipt of the BBC's services, and there is a clear perception that they are getting value for money.[46] One interesting development in the 1990s is that the extension of satellite and cable television has made consumers much more aware of what television might cost them if it were all provided commercially. In particular paying £91.50 for a licence which, in the eyes of the consumer, gives access to BBC1, BBC2, ITV and C4 seems good value when the full Sky package costs over three times as much.

The amount of revenue received from the licence fee is determined by the following factors:

(i)   The level of the fee.
(ii)   The number of households in the UK.
(iii)   The proportion of those households which owns a colour television, and (now to a near vanishing extent) the number which owns a monochrome set.
(iv)   The extent of evasion of the licence fee.
(v)   The costs of collection.

In the past fifteen years, although the government has generally attempted to keep the BBC on a tight financial rein (especially since the middle of the 1980s), the buoyancy of revenue from the licence fee has been increased by growth in the number of households, and more particularly by the penetration of colour TV sets. The number of households has risen from 20.5 million in 1980 to 22.6 million in 1990 and to

---

46. Strong evidence in favour of this can be found in Ehrenberg and Mills (1990).

22.9 million in 1995. Alongside this the penetration of colour TVs has risen from 72 per cent of all households in 1980 to 92 per cent in 1990 and to 97 per cent in 1995. Meanwhile the number of monochrome licences has been falling sharply. As a result of these factors, the number of licence payers has risen by 13 per cent, and this has been the main factor explaining the growth of licence revenue in real terms. Neither the extent of evasion, nor the costs of collection, have changed much. In fact, the licence fee remains an efficient and cheap-to-collect form of taxation. The cost of collecting the licence fee, inclusive of anti-evasion measures, was only 5.2 per cent of total licence fee revenue in 1995/6 – noticeably less than the collection costs of water rates, vehicle licences or gas, electricity and telephone charges. Moreover, evasion of the licence fee is only about 6-8 per cent.

As can be seen in Chart A, which shows licence fee income in real and nominal terms over the last 25 years, the effect of the factors mentioned above has been that licence fee revenue grew quite rapidly both in real and nominal terms up to 1985, but has risen hardly at all since then. This slow down after 1985 was the conjunction of two effects. Until the mid 1980s the number of households with colour televisions was growing rapidly (the proportion almost doubled from 1975 to 1985), but by 1985, when the proportion had reached 86 per cent, this natural buoyancy was coming to an end. Then, from 1986 onwards, the Government pegged the increase in the licence fee to the Retail Price Index (the RPI).

Chart A: Real and Nominal Licence Fee Income (£millions) 1970-96

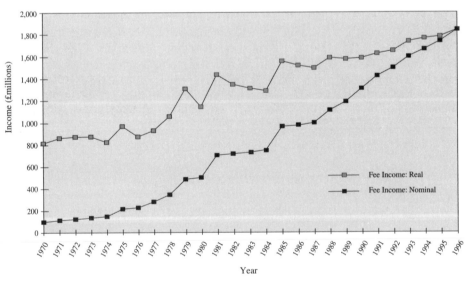

As a consequence over the last 25 years, taken as whole, licence fee receipts, deflated by the RPI, have risen by over 3 per cent per annum and this has enabled the BBC substantially to increase its provision of real services. But this overall picture covers two regimes. The first, from 1970 to 1985, saw real licence fee revenues rising by 4.4 per cent per annum, a rate which may have made life for the BBC too easy.

The second phase from 1985-96, saw real revenues rising by only 1.5 per cent per annum, which made life much more difficult, though there was almost certainly some "fat" to squeeze out of the BBC from earlier periods. The challenge for the BBC in future will be to cope with a period in which there is no natural buoyancy in real licence fee revenue, and there is no fat left to squeeze out in the provision of services. This combination, which could hit the BBC in the next decade, may prove very problematic.

This is partly because there is little logic in using the RPI as the relevant deflator when assessing the growth of licence receipts in real terms. The reason is that the BBC's costs, over the medium term, are likely to rise more rapidly than the RPI. Since the costs of the corporation are overwhelmingly labour costs and since such costs in the service sector of the economy generally rise more rapidly than the RPI, the 'real' revenue available to the BBC for the provision of services is not as great as is suggested by the 1.5 per cent per annum growth rate quoted above for the period since 1985.

There is no official index of unit labour costs in the service sector of the economy published by the Office for National Statistics, but it is possible to derive such an index from the published numbers on services output, average earnings and employment. The resulting index shows an annual average rate of increase of 5 per cent per annum in the past 10 years, compared with a rate of 4.5 per cent for the RPI.

If labour costs in the services sector are used as the relevant deflator, then real licence fee revenue from 1985-96 grew, not by 1.5 per cent per annum, but only by 1 per cent per annum. This is perhaps the best measure of what was available to increase the real provision of services by the BBC – or at least what would have been available if the corporation had achieved the undemanding target of increasing its labour costs in line with other services in the economy. As we shall see in the next section, this is a warning of what may well happen in the future if the licence fee is up-rated only in line with the RPI, while the number of households with colour television stagnates.

XII   Possibilities for the Future

It has been argued that the BBC is a 'public good', for which public finance of some sort or another is perfectly justified. We have further seen that the licence fee fulfils many, but not all, of the attributes which are to be desired in a money raising mechanism for the BBC. However, as will be seen later in this section, the licence fee also has the severe disadvantage that the present up-rating system will not allow the growth of revenue to keep pace with the growth of private sector television, so that the BBC would be condemned to fill a diminishing role in the broadcasting market unless the present system is changed. This latter problem means that it is worth considering whether a superior form of public finance is available. Several suggestions have been made, of which the following are the most frequently discussed.

First, it would be possible to fund the BBC out of general taxation. However, as discussed above, there are compelling arguments against this.

Second, it would be possible for the BBC to be given a fixed share of the revenue from another tax, such as VAT or income tax. There would be some advantages in such an approach. It would provide the BBC with a source of revenue which would grow roughly in line with nominal GDP, and this would ameliorate the recent tendency for revenue to be squeezed relative to costs. Furthermore, if it were truly automatic, it would place the subject of BBC financing outside the political arena (though how long this would last must be open to question). However, this form of finance would be likely to run into an immovable stumbling block – the entrenched opposition of the Treasury to any form of direct subvention of general tax revenue for specific spending purposes. This objection to 'hypothecation' (i.e. the tying of expenditure to a particular part of taxation) is most unlikely to change.

Third, it has been suggested that the BBC should receive a direct share of some form of revenue which is broadly related to the provision of broadcasting services, such as electricity bills. This, too, would represent a form of hypothecation, but this time of private rather than public sector revenue. It is just possible that this idea might have been viable if the electricity industry were still in the public sector, but now that it has been privatised, it is difficult to see how the government could justify taxing its output to pay for the BBC – especially when it simultaneously levies VAT on the domestic consumption of electricity. Furthermore, there is only the very loosest connection between the consumption of electricity and the use of the BBC's services, so the acceptability by the electorate of such a charge would be questionable.

Fourth, there is the possibility of levying a charge on some other form of equipment, such as videos or indeed televisions. The main case against this is that it would be likely to raise public doubts about the whole licence fee system. When the licence fee was first introduced, the BBC was a monopoly supplier, so everyone could see why they had to make a contribution towards its costs. Even now, very few people own a colour TV without making extensive use of the BBC's services, so that the link between the charge and the service remains strong. However, this is much less true of the use of videos, which are often primarily used to view non-BBC software, including the output of home video cameras. Many users may therefore be most unwilling to pay an extra charge on videos, and such an attitude could lead to widespread evasion of an annual fee. A charge made at the point of the sale would certainly be administratively feasible, but apart from the acceptability arguments already mentioned, there is the more serious extra question of why people who have already purchased videos should gain at the expense of future purchasers (especially given that two out of every three households which own a TV *already* own a video). The same argument applies to television sets since they are used in conjunction with both videos and some computer games. In view of all this, charges on videos or other similar equipment do not seem attractive.

Finally, there are two other slightly more promising possibilities. One would be a higher licence fee for digital televisions. The latter present no difficulty in principle; in much the same way as people were willing to incur a higher licence fee for colour TV because of the obvious improvement in the service, they are likely to be willing to pay extra for digital television. If this technique were to spread widely, it could solve the BBC's problem of revenue buoyancy for many years ahead. The licence fee could be up-rated in line with the RPI or some other index, and the real growth in the service would be dependent on how rapidly digital TV sets penetrated the population.

There are, however, three possible objections to this proposal. First, although digital television now looks imminent, no-one knows exactly when it will happen nor how fast the take up will be. Second, if a rapid take up of digital TV was thought to be desirable as a matter of public policy, for example, in order to spread the benefits of the "Information Society" as widely as possible, then a higher licence fee would be a disincentive. Third, at some point analogue sets will be switched off. This will be unpopular whenever it happens, but all the more so if people are thereby forced to pay a higher licence fee. In addition, once analogue is switched off a great deal of scarce spectrum will be released and the sale of this might bring substantial revenue to the Government, something that they are unlikely to want to delay. While all three of these objections have some merit (especially the need in the longer term to release spectrum), at least the first and third (and perhaps also the second to some extent) have applied in the past to the introduction of higher licence fees for television itself, and then for colour television. Nevertheless, these higher charges were widely accepted by the population, and created crucial buoyancy for BBC income.

The second possibility would be to charge a "site" licence wherever households owned more than one television. This would be similar to how computer software is sold now to companies and other large organisations. In return for paying a premium households would be able to operate as many televisions (or computers capable of receiving television) as they wished. The advantage of such a system would be twofold. First, at the same time as charging a site licence the fee for a single set could be reduced – thus reducing the cost of television to those unable to afford more than one set. Second, once the system had been introduced it would have the crucial characteristic of some income elasticity (as more households become owners of two or more sets, revenue would rise). It would also avoid the disadvantage of slowing down the switch to digital TV. On the other hand it might be administratively complicated. In particular checking on the number of sets would probably require looking in people's homes. This alone might make it very unpopular, as would the higher payment for those owning more than one television. Moreover there is no neat correlation between ownership and income so some of the households who would be forced either to reduce the number of their TVs or to pay a site licence would include some poor households who could ill afford this.

Despite the objections to each of these, there is little doubt in our minds that both of these are options which should be seriously explored for the future.

Having considered the main alternatives, it appears that the licence fee fulfils more of the 'ideal' requirements listed above than any alternative that has so far been found, and that it should remain as the most important source of BBC revenue for the foreseeable future (possibly with a top-up for digital television). However, there should be some reconsideration of the methods used for setting and up-rating the licence fee. This is for the following reasons.

First, it can be shown that up-rating the licence fee in line with changes in the RPI (the policy from 1986 to 1996) is unsatisfactory, because it inevitably results in licence fee income increasing less rapidly than the BBC's costs, thus squeezing the real level of BBC income. Broad illustrations of this problem are given in Table 1 below, which is not meant to contain precise forecasts. Over long time periods, the RPI is likely to rise broadly in line with unit labour (or wage) costs in the economy as a whole – say 2.25 per cent per annum. But, in the past, unit labour costs in "services" have risen faster than in the economy as a whole. The BBC is clearly a "service" industry and most of the BBC's costs are labour costs and so, if its revenue were forever linked to the RPI while its unit costs grew more rapidly, it would face a position of permanent decline.

Table 1: The Up-rating Problem Illustrative Long-Term Rates of Increase			
	Whole Economy % per annum	**Private Services** % per annum	**Implications for BBC** % per annum
1. Output	2.75	3.25	-0.50
2. Employment	0.50	1.50	-2.25
3. Productivity *(1-2)*	2.25	1.75	1.75
4. Wages per Head	4.50	4.50	4.50
5. Unit Wage Costs *(4-3)*	2.25	2.75	2.75
6. Wages Bill *(4+2)*	5.00	6.00	2.25
7. Retail Price Inflation *(=5)* (and BBC Revenue from Licence Fee)	2.25		

The important part of Table 1 is not the assumption about the growth of wages, nor therefore about the inflation rate over the long term. This cannot be forecast with any accuracy. What matters is the *difference* in unit wage costs (line 5).

This difference in unit wage costs between different sectors arises because productivity growth in the whole economy (say 2.25 per cent per annum) will almost certainly be faster than productivity growth in services (say 1.75 per cent per annum). In the example shown in Table 1, unit wage costs for the whole economy rise at 2.25 per cent per annum while those for private services rise at 2.75 per cent per annum. If the licence fee is up-rated in line with the RPI at 2.25 per cent per annum (line 7 in the table), it will rise by 0.5 per cent per annum less rapidly than the BBC's unit costs (line 5 in the table) – which implies that the real level of BBC's services would need to decline by that amount if the Corporation were wholly reliant on licence fee income. In other words the minus 0.5 per cent per annum shown in the top right hand corner of the table for the output of the BBC is a consequence of its real revenue rising 0.5 per cent per annum more slowly than its unit costs. The further implication is that its employment will have to fall dramatically (line2).

The *exact* numbers that we are quoting here are not crucial. What matters and what causes the problem for the BBC is that its revenue is tied inexorably to inflation whereas we think that its labour costs per unit will rise at a faster rate. The only way to square this highly unsatisfactory circle is by a mixture of reducing output and reducing employment. It is this that our table illustrates.

This squeeze on the BBC that these figures imply has some striking consequences. If the overall output of commercial broadcasting services in the private sector simply grew in line with other private services in the economy – say at 3.25 per cent per annum- then the *relative* importance of the BBC in the broadcasting market would decline by 3.75 per cent per annum. This could rapidly leave it with insufficient influence over the market to play the "quality setting" role which is so essential. Of course, the actual growth in private television services in the next decade is likely to be much greater than 3.25 per cent per annum, in which case the relative share of the BBC might fall even more rapidly than these figures suggest (as we shall see in more detail below).

Admittedly, it might be possible to offset this by increasing productivity in the BBC at a faster rate than applies to other broadcasters. The BBC's record on productivity growth in the past has been poor (especially during the years when revenue growth was so buoyant) and, until recently, can be justifiably criticised by the government. There may well therefore still be some 'fat' in the BBC, and it is possible that the present licence arrangements might lead to a squeezing of this fat – in the same way that cash limits were supposed to operate elsewhere in the public sector. Indeed there is some evidence that this has been occurring. In the last three years the BBC has achieved savings of more than 10 per cent of its revenue and it has done so while at the same time maintaining its market share. This process of raising productivity as the result of external pressure can be a healthy one – necessity is the mother of invention. However, it cannot operate for very long without eventually cutting into the bone. Indeed, most government departments found that they were into the bone after only a very few years of operating the cash limit system. After a while, public sector productivity could rise no further, and the real level of services had to fall. This is what will eventually happen to the BBC – indeed, what some observers believe was *already* happening in the late 1980s. Two pieces of research[47] both concluded that the reduction in the funding of the BBC was leading to a loss of quality and an inability to meet the full requirements of a public service broadcaster. Moreover, even if this reduction could continue, it is not clear that it is *desirable* that it should – if we want a society in which the demand for both information and education are rising faster than national income, is it not sensible that the public provision of these should also rise?

There is another reason not to over-do the search for cost cutting. Unless this is avoided an essential part of the complementarity between the BBC and the commercial sector will not work. In the late 1990s the commercial sector will be more competitive than in the past. This will put more pressure on the BBC (both directly through competition for audiences and indirectly through making it easier to use cross-industry measures of efficiency). This is desirable and itself reduces the need for other forms of regulation to control the BBC's costs. However, at the same time the BBC has to have sufficient funds, as well as sufficient certainty of future funds, to be able to innovate and take risks in ways that both challenge the commercial sector and stretch the opportunities of that sector.

Many years ago[48] it was found that a key feature in the growth of firms was to provide managers with enough spare capacity in their time for them to be able to think and plan. There is a danger, especially in the aftermath of the cost conscious and public expenditure squeezing 1980s and 1990s, that this insight will be forgotten.

It is also unlikely that there is any scope left for curtailing BBC costs by significantly reducing the relative pay offered to its staff. This would simply cause a mass exodus of people, with a sharp drop in the quality of the service. In fact the competition for staff that is already occurring following deregulation makes it much more likely that the BBC will need to increase its relative pay – the analogy with the City is suggestive. Indeed this can already be observed. As noted earlier, the real cost of talent has been rising several per cent per annum faster than inflation since at least 1990.

These considerations suggest that, if the BBC relies entirely on the licence fee for its income and the up-rating of the licence remains unchanged from the present arrangements, then the BBC will be unable to maintain the present level of service provision to absolute terms, still less in relative terms. The inevitable conclusion is that the system should be changed.

---

47. Ehrenberg and Mills (1990) and Davis (1991).
48. Penrose (1959).

XIII Alternative Up-rating Methods

One minimal way of moving in this direction would be to up-rate the licence fee each year in line with unit labour costs in the service sector of the economy as a whole. In our example, this would imply that the licence fee should be up-rated by 2.75 per cent per annum (or 0.5 per cent per annum faster than the RPI). This would allow the BBC to maintain its real level of services constant over time, provided that it could achieve productivity growth roughly in line with the average for the service sector, which seems to be a reasonable target. In the longer term, with the likely expansion of the private broadcasting sector, a more accurate indicator of the BBC's costs might be to use the change in labour costs in the private broadcasting sector as the basis for licence up-rating. This would allow the BBC to maintain the real level of its services if it could keep its productivity growth in line with the average for its own industry. This formula could not work in the near future, however, because no such index is available from the Office for National Statistics.

More Radical Alternatives

However, all this would do would be to stabilise the real level of BBC services which could be financed from the licence fee. There would be no scope for real growth, either in line with the growth in the economy, or with the growth in private broadcasting activity, which could be considerably faster. Consequently, the share of the BBC in the broadcasting market would still decline rapidly, unless alternative source of revenue could be found.

One way round this would be to up-rate the licence fee in line with the increase in overall labour costs, the "wages bill" in the private service sector (6 per cent per annum in our example), rather than the increase in unit labour costs. What this would do would be to increase the real provision of broadcasting services in the economy, as measured by an increase in the number of people who work in the industry. Hence, it would be likely that the BBC could maintain its relative position in the market even without seeking alternative sources of revenue. Although this would be ideal from the BBC's point of view, the government is not likely to welcome such a system. It would result in an annual increase in the licence fee substantially above the rate of retail price inflation. Even if consumers were willing to pay more for television on the grounds that the services it provides in terms of education and entertainment would usually be regarded as income elastic, regular increases in real terms would probably be unpopular. In addition, real increases in the licence fee would make its regressive aspects more noticeable, but this is not an insurmountable objection. The government used to include the TV licence in Supplementary Benefit payments and a similar system could be instituted in future.

Notwithstanding these arguments, it would clearly be preferable for consumers and government alike if a way could be found to increase the buoyancy of the BBC's revenue base without actually increasing the real level of the licence fee each year.

As noted above one promising way of doing this would be to levy a higher licence fee on a new product such as digital TV, thus enabling the BBC to benefit from rising income as the penetration of this product in the marketplace rises. Obviously, this approach would leave the BBC facing considerable uncertainty about the pace of increase in its revenue base, since the extent of the build-up in digital TV is not known with any precision. Estimates vary from below two million installed sets by 2005 to nearly four million.

Clearly both the extra revenue and the number of digital sets installed will depend on the extent of the extra charge made for a digital licence compared to a colour TV licence. At present, the difference between a colour and monochrome TV licence is around £60, but the consumer might not consider the quality differences between colour and digital TVS to be as obvious as the differences between colour and monochrome. So we assume for the sake of illustration that the excess on the colour licence for digital TV would be £45 a year. This would imply that, today, a digital licence would be £134.50. We further assume that with this level of extra licence fee the number of digital sets installed would be 2.7 million by 2005. Allowing for uprating between now and 2005, this would generate £149 million of extra revenue for the BBC by 2005 (about 8 per cent of today's total), which in turn would represent extra annual growth in licence revenue of about 0.75 per cent per annum, on top of what would otherwise occur.

Subsequently, the additional revenue for the BBC might expand more rapidly, since at some point the penetration of digital TV is likely to rise rapidly towards 100 per cent of the population. Assume that between 2005 and 2015, the penetration of digital TV reached 50 per cent of the population, or 13.5 million sets. This would by then generate £970 million of extra revenue per year (52 per cent of today's total), and it would boost the growth rate of real licence fee revenue from 2005-2015 by around 2 per cent per annum, compared to what would otherwise occur.

Implications of Different Up-rating Methods

If the earlier arguments about the need for the BBC to act as a guarantor of quality are persuasive, the most important factor which should determine the licence fee is the implications it carries for the BBC's market share.[49] The effects of three different up-rating methods up to the year 2000 and, beyond that, to 2005 and 2010, can be seen in Table 2. This table shows, purely illustratively, what might happen to the BBC's share of the broadcasting market if the licence fee were to be up-rated in line with the RPI at 2.25 per cent per annum (Case A), in line with total labour costs in the private services sector at 6 per cent per annum (Case B), and in line with the RPI, but including a supplement on the licence fee for digital TV as discussed above (Case C).

---

49. It is assumed throughout this section that the market share measured by viewing will move closely with shares of revenues. With the exception of the last few years this has been the case in the past and there is no reason to expect it to be markedly different in the future.

Table 2: The Implications for Market Share of Alternative Methods of Up-Rating the Licence Fee[a]

	Per cent Share Held by BBC	Per cent Share Held by Other Broadcasters
NOW (1996)[b]	43	57
Case A: In line with RPI		
2000	36 (41)	64 (59)
2005	29 (38)	71 (62)
2010	22 (35)	78 (65)
Case B: In line with Labour Costs		
2000	40 (44)	60 (56)
2005	36 (46)	64 (54)
2010	32 (47)	68 (53)
Case C: In line with RPI plus digital supplement		
2000	37 (41)	63 (59)
2005	30 (39)	70 (61)
2010	25 (39)	75 (61)

Notes

(a) In all three cases the licence fee is assumed to grow by approximately one per cent per annum because of natural buoyancy. The main figures in the table show the effects of using the growth of output for other broadcasters of 8 per cent per annum. The figures in brackets assume growth of 3.25 per cent per annum for other broadcasters. None of the figures is intended to be more precise than the discussion in the text.

(b) Shares of revenue in 1996. Licence fee revenue is measured net of the costs of collection.

The numbers given in Table 2 are on two different bases. First, the main numbers show the effect of assuming that the growth in private TV services is around 8 per cent per annum, thus allowing for the explosive growth which is occurring in this sector at present. Second, the figures in parentheses show what might happen if the output of private broadcasters increased in line with other private services at 3.25 per cent per annum. The only additional assumption incorporated in this table is that the licence fee is taken to have a natural buoyancy of about one per cent per annum, in line with the forecast growth in the number of households.

On these assumptions the effect of linking the value of licence fee to the RPI (Case A) is that the BBC share of the market would shrink to 36 per cent by the year 2000 and to a only 29 per cent by 2005. In Case B (uprating in line with wage costs), the BBC's market share shrinks much more slowly to 40 per cent by the year 2000 and to 36 per cent by 2005. In Case C (the RPI plus digital supplement), the BBC's market share declines to 37 per cent in 2000 and 30 per cent in 2005. This represents an intermediate case.

In each of our 3 main cases, the share of the BBC in the broadcasting market therefore continues to fall. Of course, the table could be too pessimistic if broadcasting share is not correlated with real expenditure in future, or if the growth in private broadcasting is lower than the 8 per cent per annum assumed in our main case. (See the figures in parentheses.)

The point to be emphasised, however, is not the precise figures. The future will undoubtedly turn out somewhat different from any of the pictures given here. The point is that, whatever the exact figures, tying the licence fee to the RPI implies a continuing fall in the BBC's market share. This immediately raises two critical questions. First, how long will it be until the BBC is too small to play the "quality-setting" role that is so essential. Second, how large does the BBC need to be to influence the market?

It is not possible to give precise answers to these questions. Nevertheless, there are three pieces of evidence on which to draw. First, most countries which have licence fees as a source of public broadcasting revenue these broadcasters have market shares of viewing of at least 25 per cent, and the great majority exceed 40 per cent. It is possible that the licence fee is only acceptable if a large number of the public watch public broadcasting for a significant amount of time. Moreover, at some point as the share falls, the claim of the public service broadcaster to be meeting the needs of the community is no longer sustainable. Any claim to universality must eventually collapse. For this reason, also, the licence fee might become indefensible.

Second, there is some indirect evidence from the industrial economics literature. Various authors have measured the point at which the four largest firms in an industry recognised their inter-dependence. An early study[50] found a critical level of market share at 55 per cent, but subsequent studies had estimates of the critical level varying from as high as 59 per cent to as low as 45 per cent.[51] Of course, the BBC as a single organisation may be able to be smaller than this and still be an important player. Also the ways in which the BBC is required to influence the market are not directly comparable to the pricing and profit maximising considerations of most industrial markets. Nevertheless, such findings suggest, even if only weakly, that the BBC could not become a great deal smaller and still be a powerful influence.

Third, later work[52] found that, in order to influence a market, firms need a larger market share if they used to be small and are expanding than if they used to be large and are contracting. This would help to explain why earlier research had found such a spread of results about the level at which inter-dependence was recognised.

Again it is necessary to be extremely cautious in applying these results to broadcasting, but the important implication of the later work, which accords with common sense, is that, if the BBC became too small to act as the "quality setter",

---

50. Meehan and Duchesneau (1973).

51. Dalton and Penn (1976) found evidence for a break at 45 per cent, White (1976) at between 56 per cent and 59 per cent and Sant (1978) at 47 per cent.

52. Bradburd and Mead Over (1981).

it would then be much more difficult to re-establish this role. The relationship both between the public and the BBC and between the BBC and the commercial sector is one which depends heavily on reputation. Once destroyed it would not be easily rebuilt.

Taken together these three points suggest, even if only tentatively, that there would be real dangers for the quality of UK broadcasting if the BBC were to be pushed down to, say, 25-30 per cent of the market. Moreover, on some readings of the evidence above, it would be wise to sustain the market share at a higher level.

XIV Summary and Conclusions

Who needs public service broadcasting? The answer is that we all do and that the new technology *increases*, not *decreases*, this need. The reasons are, first, that there is a real danger that if broadcasting were left just to the market it would become excessively concentrated; second, that even if this were not the case, commercial broadcasting on its own would fail to produce the form of broadcasting which people individually or citizens and voters collectively require; and, third, that there is no set of rules or regulations or laws which could entirely correct the deficiencies of a commercial system. This is for the simple but powerful reason that rules are necessarily negative. They have the capacity only to stop the undesirable. They cannot promote the desirable.

The only way to counteract fully the deficiencies of a purely commercial system is through the existence of a broadcaster which has as its driving force the ethos of public service broadcasting.

Such a public service broadcaster would fulfil three crucial and inter-related roles. First, it would act as a counterweight to possible monopolisation of ownership and yet fragmentation of audiences in the private sector. Second, because its *purposes* were different, it would *widen* the choice that consumers individually and collectively would face. Third, provided it were large enough, it would have a positive influence on the quality and behaviour of the whole system. In brief, such a public service broadcaster is not an optional add-on, but central to the health of all broadcasting. The BBC does not have a *right* to exist, but it does have *purposes for its existence.*

There could be more than one such public service broadcaster – since competition *within* the public sector is also healthy. However, if so, at least one of them has to be vertically integrated. This follows first from the need for public service broadcasting to be concerned with the full range of broadcasting (training, production, scheduling and broadcasting) and, second, from the fact that public services values and the commitment to quality can only be maintained, developed and passed on within an institutional framework that persists.

Equally important is that, alongside any public service broadcaster, there should be an active commercial sector. Each improves the other. The commercial sector keeps the public sector competitive, the public sector raises quality and keeps the commercial sector honest. Moreover, the commercial sector should include both broadcasters and independent producers and, as now, the independents should supply programmes both to the commercial sectors and to the PSBs. This intelligent mix is what the UK has already and it should be continued – not thrown away just when it is even more required.

At the centre of this mix is the public service broadcaster (or broadcasters) providing universal coverage, creating the space for public debate and setting standards for all. It is not possible to say *precisely* how large a public service

63

broadcaster has to be to play this role. Nevertheless, the evidence from other industries and other countries suggests that it would be dangerous to push the public service broadcaster down to, very approximately, 25-30 per cent of the market. Moreover, any decision about the future level of funding must take account of the new environment of the 1990s. In the past the commercial sector was constrained from following purely commercial considerations by public service obligations. These constraints will apply less in the future both because of de-regulation and because, via globalisation and other factors, technical change is making any regulation less effective. At the same time, because of the greater competition for scarce skills, less of the staff of the commercial sector are likely to have a prior spell of training with the BBC. There will therefore be a lower supply of people committed to high quality, good broadcasting practices and public service ideals. Both of these factors mean that in order to have even the same influence as in the past, the BBC would need to have a larger market share not a smaller one.

It is in the light of this need to guarantee quality that the scale of future financial arrangements should be decided – not the other way round.

As far as the source of finance is concerned, there is nothing better than the continuation of the licence fee. However, it should *not* be related to the RPI as at present. Broadcasting costs will grow faster than retail price inflation and, even over a relatively short period, will squeeze the BBC too much for it to be able to play the "quality setting" role that is required.

Instead of the present system, in the immediate future, and as a minimum change, the basis for up-rating the licence fee should be changed from the RPI to the increase in unit labour costs in the private service sector. At a later date, if private broadcasting becomes large enough to provide a useful comparison, the basis should be changed to the increase in unit labour costs for the industry itself. However, even this will imply a fall in the *relative* share of the BBC. The only way to avoid this would be to seek to tie the licence fee to the increase in *overall* labour costs in broadcasting (even though this may appear too generous to an organisation which has not in the past been particularly good at achieving high rates of productivity growth).

Faced with a squeeze on its relative position the BBC should *not* seek to expand commercial income because the scope for doing so without prejudicing the public service role is extremely limited. The BBC can either maximise profits, or it can seek to maximise the effectiveness of its public service broadcasting. It cannot maximise both simultaneously. Rather than have this confused situation two significant changes should be considered. Either a higher licence fee should be charged for digital TV sets or some form of "site" licence should be introduced. Each of these would give the licence fee the buoyancy it requires.

One final point remains to be made. The BBC exists, does its job to international acclaim, and is, in general, highly appreciated at home. It would seem crazy, even just on insurance grounds, to start running it down *before* the effects of the new technologies and the de-regulation have come into anything like their full effect. If the BBC did not exist, it ought to be created with the utmost urgency. But endless experience demonstrates that the process of creation and destruction are *not* symmetrical. It would take a very brave or dogmatic policy-maker to be entirely sure that the arguments presented here will turn out to be wrong, and that the BBC will not be needed in the new environment. But once the BBC is destroyed, or fatally weakened, there may be no going back. It would be very difficult to re-create seventy-five years of public broadcasting culture once it had disappeared.

Bibliography

Arrow, K. (1962) "Economic Welfare and the Allocation of Resources for Invention" in *The Rate and Direction of Inventive Activity: Economic and Social Factors* Princeton University Press

Bertelsmann Foundation (1995) *Television Requires Responsibility* Bertelsmann Foundation Publishers, Guetersloh, Germany

Bradburd, R.M. and A. Mead Over, Jr. (1981) "Organisational Costs, 'Sticky Equilibria', and Critical Levels of Concentration", *Review of Economics and Statistics*

Cox, C. and H. Kreigbaum (1989) *Innovation and Industrial Strength in the UK, West Germany, United States and Japan* Policy Studies Institute, London

Dalton, J.E. and D.W. Penn (1976) "The Concentration-Profitability Relationship: Is There a Critical Concentration Ratio?" *Journal of Industrial Economics*, pp133-142

Davis, J. (1991) *TV: UK Special Report* Knowledge Research, Peterborough

DTI (1990) *Proceedings of a Conference on Innovation and Short-termism, 25 June 1990* The DTI Innovation Advisory Board in association with Financial Times Conferences

Ehrenberg, A. and P. Mills (1990) *Viewers' Willingness to Pay: A Research Report* International Thompson Business Publishing, London

Finegold, D. and D. Soskice (1988) "The Failure of Training In Britain", *Oxford Review of Economic Policy* Vol. 4, No. 3

Forbes, J. (1989) "France:Modernisation Across the Spectrum" in G. Nowell-Smith (ed.) *The European Experience* British Film Institute, London

Gallucci, C. (1994) "How many votes did TV change?" *L'Espresso* 11 November

Graham, A. (1995). "Public policy and the information superhighway: The scope for strategic intervention, co-ordination and top-slicing" In R. Collins and J. Purnell (eds.) *Managing the Information Society* London: IPPR.

Graham, A. (1996) *Evidence to the House of Lords Select Committee on Science and Technology, Information Society: Agenda for Action in the UK – Evidence received after 31 March 1996* House of Lords Paper 77-II

Graham, A. (1997) *Public Policy and Electronic Programme Guides: A Response to Oftel and to the Independent Television Commission*, mimeo

Greenhalgh, C. (1989) *Employment and Structural Change in Britain: Trends and Policy Options* Employment Institute, London

Harding, R. (1985) "Australia: Broadcasting in the Political Battle" in R. Kuhn (ed.) *The Politics of Broadcasting* Croom Helm, London

Katz, M. and J. Ordover (1990) "R&D Cooperation and Competition" *Brookings Papers on Microeconomics*

Lange, B-P. and R. Woldt (1995) in Bertelsmann Foundation *Television Requires Responsibility*, Guetersloh, Germany

Madge, T. (1989) *Beyond the BBC: Broadcasters and the Public in the 1980s* Macmillan, London

Mayer, C. and I. Alexander (1990) *Banks and Securities Markets: Corporate Financing in Germany and the UK* Centre for Economic Policy Research Discussion Paper No. 433

Meehan, J.W. and T.D. Duchesneau (1973) "The Critical Level of Concentration: An Empirical Analysis" *Journal of Industrial Economics* 22, pp21-35

Mepham, J. (1989) "The Ethics of Quality in Television." in G. Mulgan (ed.) *The Question of Quality* British Film Institute, London

Mowery, D.C. (1986) "Industrial Research 1900-1950" in B. Elbaum and W. Lazonick (eds.) *The Decline of the British Economy* Oxford University Press

NEDC (1983) *Innovation in the UK* National Economic Development Office, London

Noam, E.M. et al (1995) "The United States of America" in Bertelsmann Foundation *Television Requires Responsibility*, Guetersloh, Germany

Oftel (1996) *Consultative Document on Conditional Access*. December

Peacock Committee (1986) *Report of the Committee On Financing the BBC* Cmnd. 9824. London, HMSO

Penrose, E.T. (1959) *The Theory of the Growth of the Firm* Blackwell, Oxford

Rovizzi, L. and D. Thompson (1991) *Price-Cap Regulated Public Utilities and Quality Regulation in the UK* Centre for Business Strategy, Working Paper Series No 111, London Business School

Sant, D.T. (1978) *A Polynomial Approximation for Switching Regressions with Applications to Market Structure-Performance Studies* Federal Trade Commission staff working paper (Washington, D.C.: Federal Trade Commission, February)

White, L.J. (1976) "Searching for the Critical Industrial Concentration Ratio", in S. Goldfeld and R. E. Quandt (eds.) *Studies in Non-Linear Estimation* Cambridge, MA: Ballinger

Williams, R. (1996) *Normal Service Won't Be Resumed: The Future of Public Broadcasting* Allen & Unwin, Australia